T0064260

ENHANCING EMPLOYABILITY IN EDUCATION

ENHANCING EMPLOYABILITY IN EDUCATION

DR. TILAK KUMAR SHARMA

ELT Consultant & Teacher Trainer
Ex-IELTS Examiner, British Council
Project Director. HRE, Assam Chapter
Retired Professor, Post Graduate Training College, Jorhat
Dean, University of Science and Technology, Meghalaya

PARTRIDGE
A Penguin Random House Company

To order additional copies of this book, contact
Partridge India
000 800 10062 62
orders.india@partridgepublishing.com

www.partridgepublishing.com/india

CONTENTS

Dedicated to –

Prof. Prasanna Kumar Barua [Late]
who was my Guru and colleague.

FOREWORD

Dr. Tilak's analytical study on "Enhancing Employability in Education" is a discriminating and surprising work of this category in the history of vocational education in Assam, nay, in the whole country I have come across so far.

The work exposes the concept of vocational education in its totality. Enlightening and systematic presentation of chronological development of vocational training in the State depicts the writer's trait as a silent observer of what has been happening in the field of vocational education from a considerable early period in this part of the country.

It is an extremely good piece of writing, knowledgeable and informative and it is hoped that it will prove increasingly beneficial to students, teachers and researchers for all time to come.

Dr. Sarma, who is teaching at the Post Graduate Training College, Jorhat is a teacher par excellence and I had some wonderful moments discussing educational issues with him, particularly the classroom related problems. He is a rare master in Classroom Management.

I have an aspiration that given a high-quality work environment and opportunity Dr Tilak can make great things happen in the field of teaching and learning.

I wish Dr Tilak Sarma all success in his endeavours and hope to see him come up with more productive and creative writing in future.

Prasanna Kumar Barua

Date 26 September 2010   Tarajan, Jorhat. (Assam)

PREFACE

If we say that education is the basic right of every individual, it also implies that every individual has the basic right to be engaged in some useful trade or occupation after finishing education. The purpose of this comprehensive work is to focus on the importance of providing necessary skills to students to make them truly employable and useful for the nation. A comparative study has also been attempted between regular vocational programs and social fairness and job reliability and its effect in building up the career of the present generation youngsters. Here we are just trying to look into what best can be done to promote individual talent and skills to realize his or her potential role for the growth and development of the nation.

This was my first attempt in writing something of this nature which I had started way back in the eighties. But due to health related issues, the work was left half done. I started it afresh in the nineties and completed a couple of chapters, but health conditions during that period became a serious impediment to the completion of the task at one go. Now time has considerably changed and in spite of the fact that the content might demand some modifications, I have tried to complete the work keeping the content and volume at the same level.

All through the post-independence period there have been numerous attempts to reform the Indian vocational education system and make it more appropriate and relevant. The list of vocational education policy reforms that have been attempted over the last 60 plus years is, to a certain extent, wide and comprehensive. Standards have not moved up but efforts have been made to go forward with market-oriented reforms to the vocational education system. This study mainly focuses on the present vocational education system with the help of some analytical data and also proposes certain policy interventions in the parallel education system.

The primary intention of this publication, however, is to assess and describe the need for introducing Vocational education with a little more seriousness than ever before and to suggest ideas for establishing a Vocational University with a difference. The idea is also to summarize the present state and national Vocational Education scenario and its problems. I also intend to hint upon some recommendation for policies to be implemented at State Level and suggest possible measures to make vocational courses more relevant to the need of the time.

Vocational Education, if properly structured and systematically implemented, will definitely go a long way in shaping the destiny of the nation. Students have, in the meanwhile, understood the value and importance of such courses in contrast to general courses, which have limited job avenues and restricted salary structure. The question then arises as to

❖ Why universities have tremendously failed to give an added impetus to these courses?
   and
❖ Why it seems as if the programs are still in the initial stage of experimentation in the North Eastern States particularly in the State of Assam?

Expert committees should be immediately instituted not only at the state level but also at the national level for an ex-post evaluation of the vocational education programs so far implemented. This will help in arriving at a proper analysis of the whole situation and provide effective feedback, which will determine the nature of the follow-up action to be taken to bring about a thorough and absolute change in the whole system for a better future of government owned institutions and university affiliated colleges. The present monograph is an evaluative study of the different aspects of existing vocational courses in these institutions. Attempt has been made to concentrate on the following areas:

- o Deliberation on the vocational courses suggested by the Ministry of Education.
- o Assessment of the demand for vocational skills for better job performance.
- o Evaluation of experiments conducted in the field of vocational education and accomplishments.
- o Evaluation of problems and challenges.
- o Course analysis and recommendations.

A comparative study has also been attempted between regular vocational programs and social fairness and job reliability and its effect in building up the career of the present generation youngsters.

Keeping this larger context in mind, I have tried to concentrate on three key issues:-

1. The primary objective is to put together the result of an inadvertent study of the relationship between the general education and vocational education, and its impact on economic system and national development, demonstrating thereby that vocationalization has

much to offer in terms of exploring alternative, more cost effective and reasonably benign forms of economic production.

2. The second endeavor is to consider the possibility of the application of these issues in secondary schools/ colleges and the existing ITIs that have the potential to impart a remarkable vocational education program that will definitely be acknowledged some day; but have deplorably failed to sustain the required standard and dignity over the years since its glorious inception.

3. I've also tried to focus on the initiatives, challenges and the process of implementation of various projects and schemes undertaken by the government at different times in a bid to enhance employability. The objective is to explore into the output and its impact on the workforce plus the growth and development of the country.

Vocationalisation and its specific manifestation in schools in the form of vocational education programs has generally been defined and practiced as skill training for future employment. To illustrate the genuineness and obvious applicability of this conception in real context, I have made a conscious effort to explore the chronological development of Vocational Training in the State of Assam in Eastern India, and the way it expanded under difficult social and material conditions; but which is yet to develop into a worth mentioning vocational program to make our future generation truly employable.

I can't but acknowledge my gratitude to the Education Department, Government of Assam for giving me the opportunity to conduct this study. I am grateful to the Directorate, Technical Education as well as the Directorate Vocational Educational for extending their co-operation helping me by furnishing the required information for the study. I convey my heartfelt gratitude to Prasanta Kumar Baruah, Ex-Director of Employment and Craftsman Training, Assam and Nokul Chandra Bordoloi, Senior Supervisor, I.T.I. Jorhat (Assam) for helping me in all possible ways by providing necessary information as and when required. I would be doing injustice to my work if I fail to mention that it was his continued support, which led to the publication of this monograph. I can't but also remain indebted to Late Prasanna Kumar Barua, Ex-Deputy Director, SCERT, Assam, who in spite of his busy schedule took the trouble to go through the preliminary draft of this monograph and offered necessary comments and suggestions on it. He has been kind enough to write a foreword to this work by highlighting some of the need-based issues of the hour. I am really honored to get his support and encouragement and wish he were alive today to see this work published.

Above all, I attribute my success to Md. Mohobobul Hoque Chancellor, USTM and Ajmal Borbhuyan, Registrar, Regional Institute of Science and Technology, Meghalaya who had been a great source of strength and inspiration for my work.

Finally however, I also owe my success to my wife Ira as well as my two daughters, Paromita and Parismita, who supported and inspired me all through.

Tilak Kumar Sharma

1

ASPECTS OF EMPLOYABILITY

The Concept defined

Despite the fact that there is no singular definition of employability, an analytical study in the context of skill-based education and job prospect suggests that employability basically refers to a compilation of essential qualities that demands the perfection in respect of knowledge, expertise and attitude which is crucial for success in any workplace. It refers to a person's competence to get employed and retain that employment on the basis of knowledge and expertise they have acquired. The ability to present the acquired skills to employers and the context within which they seek employment counts a lot. Context denotes individual conditions and job environment. As such employability is greatly affected by a series of factors which are often beyond the intellectual capacity and power of the individual. Such factors have been very technically termed as supply-side and demand-side factors

In a broader perspective, it speaks of:

- the flair and aptness to gain initial employment.
- the aptitude to maintain employment and make 'transitions' between jobs and roles within the same organization to fulfill emerging job requirements, and

1

- the aptness to obtain fresh employment if required, and the ability to cope with abrupt employment transitions within the organization or between different organizations.

Consequently, it is to be ensured that the requisite 'key skills', career counseling and a clear perception about the world of work are embedded in the vocational education system.

It is also indicates:

- the quality of such work or employment. People may be able to obtain work but it may be below their level of skill, or the salary may be poor. It may also be somewhat undesirable or unsustainable kind of a job.
- The dexterity and potentiality of gaining and maintaining productive work over the period of one's working life.

The modern concept of employability has also been determined by certain variables like:

- the varying nature in public employment policy where increasing emphasis is being given to skills-based solutions to economic competition and work-based solutions to social deprivation.
- the hypothetical closing stages of 'careers' and lifetime job security, which evidently apply to a marginal number of the workforce. With the change of time greater uncertainty among employers is evidently perceived in terms of the levels and types of jobs they will have in the future.

Employability, from what has been discussed above, is a set of essential abilities that necessitate the development of skilled proficient workers and updated technical know-how as well as positive attitude which is indispensable for success in any place of work nowadays.

Constituents of employability

This suggests that we can split the whole concept into four main constituents in respect of individual's employability: the first three can be said to relate to three important concepts which is true to all trades; e.g.

- Production,
- Marketing and
- Sales, and the fourth is the
- Marketplace

The first three i.e., Production, Marketing and Sales can be said to relate to three distinct concepts which is true to all trades. One is an incomplete notion without the other. The fourth constituent incorporates the first three and it is this field in which they all operate. This makes it evidently clear that the four constituents make a complete whole. Another way of saying it is that to get hold of the marketplace one must have properly mastered the technicalities of PMS.

1. Plus points

An individual's 'employability' can preferably be rated on the basis of certain 'plus points' which is a composite of the following fundamental qualities:

- knowledge (i.e. what they know or the amount of information they have acquired from study),
- skills (what they can do with what they know) and
- approaches (how they accept and perform the task in hand i.e., how they use their knowledge to perform a particular task).

- attitudes (the way they think and feel about the task in hand and the people they work with)

There is a number of additional plus points as well, which act as an all-inclusive taxonomy in this area to prepare a strong foundation for employability:

- 'basic plus points' such as
  - basic skills and essential personal attributes (such as sincerity, reliability and integrity).
- 'Core plus points' such as
  - occupational specific skills (all levels),
  - generic or key skills (i.e., communication and problem solving) and
  - key personal attributes (i.e., motivation, creativity and initiative),
- 'Higher plus points' involving
  - skills which help contribute to organizational performance. For example - team work, self-management, creative awareness, acutely conscious of effectual productivity etc.

Further key points which provide a strong base to employability are:-

- the importance of transferability of the acquired skills from one occupational context to another and
- the softer attitudinal skills employers look for in selecting employees.

Merely being in possession of employer-relevant knowledge, skills and attitudes is not enough for an individual to consider himself 'self-sufficient' in the modern employment market. People also need the capability to exploit their resources, to market them and sell them. The course of action should be apparently clear and comprehensive.

2. Course of action

Course of action involves a co-related set of abilities which are commonly termed as Career management skills and life skills. Life skills are performance abilities which basically refer to a set of human skills or abilities acquired through education or direct experience that are used to handle issues and problems commonly encountered in real life. The subject varies greatly depending on social standards and community expectations. Life skills are commonly identified as

- self-awareness (i.e. diagnosing occupational interests and abilities),
- opportunity awareness (knowing what work opportunities exist and their entry requirements i.e. job market knowledge),
- decision-making skills (to develop a strategy of getting from where you are to where you want to be) and
- maneuver skills (to manage, control or influence a situation in a skillful manner).

Other essential skills to consider are:

- Job search skills — i.e. finding suitable jobs. Access to formal and informal networks is an important component of job search and employability.
- Strategic approach — being adaptable to employment market developments and realistic about employment market opportunities, and being occupation wise and location wise mobile.

The extent to which an individual is aware of what they possess in terms of knowledge, skills and attitudes and its relevance to the employment opportunities available may affect their willingness to undertake training and other activities. The training and the activities referred to, cannot but be preferably designed to upgrade the existing skills and abilities of the prospective individual to be truly employable.

Significantly, the ability to realize or actualize 'employability' plus points depends on the individual's personal and external circumstances and the inter-relationship between the two. This includes:

- Personal circumstances — home conditions i.e., concerned responsibilities of kith and kin, physical and mental abilities as well as knowledge acquired through education and real-life experience.
- External factors i.e., macro-economic demand and the pattern and level of job openings in the employment market, employment market regulation and benefit rules; and employer recruitment policies and selection procedures.

All these aspects can tremendously affect their aptitude to hunt for different opportunities and will invariably vary during an individual's life cycle.

3. Priorities of action

For raising the skill profile of the existing workforce, especially at lower levels to boost flexibility and competitiveness, there are a number of potential priority groups, the most significant among them being —

- employment market entrants
- employment market re-entrants
- disadvantaged groups
- insecure or under-utilized employees

Depending on group requirements and circumstances different policies may need to be short-listed on priority basis.

For employers the priorities might be to help key clusters of staff to develop the plus points which have overt, immediate value to the organization as well as those transferable ones which have wider, longer term control. In so doing it brings about a sense of security, encouraging commitment, promoting enthusiasm, risk-taking and flexibility among employees.

Studies have revealed that there is a great amount of skills gap in the candidates seeking employment after their diploma or degree. It suggests that commercial awareness, leadership qualities, commitment and drive, problem solving qualities and knowledge base are some of the vital areas which are mostly in need of attention.

For the individual, the need in to-days context is to boost those aspects of their employability which will mainly enhance their opportunities in the light of their circumstances. However, what the individual believes to be most important may not necessarily match with the views of the employer. There is always a variation; and there are situations where disparity and discrepancies cannot be ruled out.

Need for streamlining policies affecting employability

Employability skills are, by and large, considered vitally essential credentials for many job positions and for this reason it is said to provide a basis for analyzing the policies affecting the employability of certain groups – particularly those who belong to 16-17 age groups and are fresh diploma holders or school pass outs. Conversely, some major policy initiatives with a new vision on employability may be devised. The government initiative in this pursuit is of paramount importance and the new policy may be aimed:

- more at the development and accreditation of knowledge and vocational skills than at the 'softer' skills and attitudes
- more on the demonstration of fundamental advantages/resources than their operation/utilization — particularly for adults. There seems to be a continuous demand for better provision of a careers education and guidance service for adults
- more at individuals looking to cross the threshold of the employment market i.e.,. entry from education or unemployment
- more on the individual and the supply side, than on employers and the demand side i.e., the employment market related factors.

This policy orientation, if judiciously devised, may eliminate a variety of factors such as

- difficulties in defining, assessing and verifying 'soft skills', and
- difficulties identifying and accessing specific groups of employees at which to target limited resources.

Thus some key questions for future policy interventions centre round the identification of:

- the priority groups
- the essentially serious gaps for priority groups identified and which category of resources, dimensions of operation or presentational skills they relate to
- the remedial measures to eliminate the gaps and
- the objectives for streamlining policies to enhance employability

Interventions and crisis will be there, they just need to be properly assessed and evaluated and remedied so that we can look forward to further improvements. This will help to decide whether to continue with, change or stop such interventions. And if decided, how to stop it will still be a fundamentally vital issue. Varied measures need to be considered for appraisal of the developments.

1. <u>Potential measures</u> — The scope of these measures is quite comprehensive as they include factors relating to input measures, e.g.
   - possession of vocational qualifications, or
   - receiving career management training;
2. <u>Perception measures</u> – It takes into account
   - the analytic opinion of employers and
   - the attitude and outlook of the prospective workforce;
3. <u>Outcome measures</u> – It studies 'measurements of success' i.e., the speed at which people are able to get jobs or 'measurements of failure', e.g.
   - the numbers or proportion of people having difficulty in finding or retaining the job, or
   - the number of job changes. Every aspect relating to need of change, however, needs to be distinctly spelt out.

Obviously, the whole process should be flexible and there should be abundant scope for a combination of all the three measures. Whatever course is chosen, it is important to —

- take into account the overall state of the employment market and the way it changes
- take account of any impediments and its effect on the system,
- assess true accompaniments and be extremely positive in attitude and approach.

++++++++++++++++++++

II

TECHNICAL AND VOCATIONAL EDUCATION AND TRAINING
[Issues and Presumptions]

Basically, Technical and Vocational Education is education based on occupation or employment. It is also called Technical and Vocational Education and Training (TVET) and it has the responsibility to train and prepare people and make them employable for specific trades. The role of Vocational Education in facilitating social and economic advancement has been extensively recognized since long. It develops functional and analytical aptitude and thereby opens up opportunities for individuals to achieve greater access to employment markets and achievements in life. A blacksmith is a traditional tradesman but when he is well-trained in **FORGER AND HEAT TREATER** he falls in the engineering category of mechanical trade. He is then highly employable and has a distinct position of his own in the job market.

Technical and Vocational Education and Training consists of practical and useful programs through which one gains knowledge, skills and experience directly linked to a career in future. It trains and prepares trainees for jobs that are based on manual or practical activities entirely linked to a specific trade, <u>occupation</u>, or <u>vocation</u> and also offers better employment opportunities. The trainee is expected to develop expertise in his field of study so that he becomes fit for a sustainable employment. Technical and vocational education helps students to be trained and skilled and the trainings they receive are parallel to other conventional courses of study like bachelor and master courses in the science stream. But Technical and Vocational education is preferably classified as imparting <u>procedural knowledge</u> and is offered at the <u>secondary</u> or <u>post-secondary</u> level and is interrelated with the <u>apprenticeship</u> system.

Time management and meeting deadlines play an important role in the process of achieving success in a vocational course and during their studies students normally produce a portfolio of verified evidence in the form of report writings, preparing charts and models, drawings, video presentations and apprenticeships, which are taken as a demonstration of students' capabilities for a job. After finishing the courses, students are often offered placements in respective fields. Vocational trainings in a way give students some amount of work related experience that many employers look for. The main objective of technical and vocational education at all levels of teaching whatsoever has traditionally been the preparation of youth for a suitable and sustainable employment.

We know that modern education was introduced in India as a result of the Lord McCauley's Minute in 1835 and it was systematically structured and expanded on the basis of the epoch-making Wood's Dispatch of 1854. Initially its main objective was confined to training Indians to occupy subordinate positions in Government service to help the British rulers in the administrative affairs of the country. Education imparted in schools was, to a large extent, academic and general in nature. Wood's dispatch had insisted on vocationalisation of education but for the next fifty years or so nothing was practically done to set things right in that line.

Over the ages, people not only in the State of Assam, but to a certain extent, in other parts of the country as well, continued to show total disregard for vocational education. It is only recently that a perceptible change has been noticed in almost everybody's attitude towards technical and vocational education; and attempts are being made to prioritize this system of education for enhancing the scope of employability for educated graduates and under-graduates. Courses are being updated and re-structured as to incorporate vocational subjects in the syllabus even for higher classes. But uncertainties still hover in the minds of educationists and planners whenever they have to make a choice in respect of the following important question.

**How much of higher education should be general plus liberal and how much vocational?

The question of balancing education between these two spheres continues to confront most of us even today. To find an answer to this question in Indian context, one has to make an intensive study of the overall development of the country. India as it is, the so-called developing country, cannot afford to place continued emphasis on liberal education. It should rather increasingly concentrate on making education as vocational as practicable and see that it does not, as usual, receive the same cool response. The planners at the government level as well as educationists and the intelligentsia will have to play a considerably significant role in this regard. Else, education will not be able to keep at par with the national goals of development. Experience shows that continued emphasis on liberal education has given rise to certain enigmatic issues –

> ➢ It has alarmingly swelled the number of the unemployed
> ➢ It has caused discontentment and unrest at both fronts – the students as well as the teaching community.
> ➢ It has distorted all calculations and deranged every planned strategy of development.
> ➢ It has pushed the system of education towards a state of chaos beyond all possible limits.

In spite of the fact that we have made rapid strides in literacy and education, there are certain points, which have to be taken rather seriously to make education more relevant and competitive in the present context. Since independence, India has built the third largest tertiary educational system in the world and yet it is shocking that we still lack the vision and impetus to make education essentially career-oriented as to provide suitable employment opportunities or make it feasible for the educated youths to be self-employed. It is evident that the system has tremendously failed to

a) generate endeavor and a spirit of initiative.
b) produce sincere and dedicated professionals.
c) produce honest and self-dependant citizens infused with the spirit that there could be no alternative to work culture, which can make the nation rich and affluent.
d) eradicate narrow sentiments and develop healthy and optimistic attitude in the people
e) make education life-related and job-oriented

This failure may perhaps be ascribed to the most enduring belief based on the misconceived notion that vocational education is primarily intended only for the potential dropouts after the school final or +2 or other students with special needs and special career choices. And the most wonderful thing is that this belief was confined not only among students and parents but educators and policy makers also shared the same view. But this has proved far from truth with the change of time and experience. No one can deny the fact that almost every high school student today is familiar with the traditional vocational courses and will be willing to take a course, which can provide immediate and perhaps better job opportunity after he passes out. The other way, he may even go for it if he is just guaranteed a vocational educational scholarship. And he has good reason to think that way because there are ample scopes for post secondary vocational education scholarships. Many students coming from vocational schools seek admission at the +2 level at about the same rate as any other high school pass outs and are found to be equally proficient in their studies; so it is unfair to level a section of students as potentially weak in studies. It is evidently clear from recent studies that vocational graduates are more employable and earn more than their non-vocational counterparts. This is because of the fact that generic technical skills and occupation specific skills, which are acquired during the course is expected to increase job productivity. Transfer of learning is positive and it tremendously helps in skill transfer thereby rendering quality management and job stability.

What reinforces the traditional negative image of vocational education is the related set of beliefs about the job market. It has always been thought and assumed that academic programs are superior to technical training. It is this assumption, which has led the parents to develop the tendency to prefer their children go for a 3-year degree course after Plus 2, which, it is presumed, assures them a job at least. Students themselves would definitely prefer to take up a course of their choice but which should, however, guarantee them a job, a regular pay and a status. A degree in a general academic course was expected to provide all this till very recent time. It is only a new millennium thought that industries would suffer tremendously in the coming decades due to shortages of scientists, engineers, economists and mathematicians. This is nothing but a raft of common misconceptions about vocational education, the job market and the three-year college degree. Vocational Education, as the very name suggests, often tends to invoke an auto-negative response. But it is also true that there are people with positive attitude towards many of the traditional aspects of vocational education.

Considering the fact that education is the means for bringing effectual socio-economic transformation in a society; various measures are being taken to enhance the employability of education and to make it truly productive. One such measure is the introduction of vocational / technical education in a new form i.e., an inclusive vocational education and it is believed that such a system of education can help out in realizing the values of equality, social justice and Democracy, which in turn will prove instrumental in creating a just and humane society.

The hard reality in the present contexts is that majority of employment opportunities are in the private sector and the sector is very choosy and stringent. Private sectors look only for candidates who possess skill competencies required by it and its necessities continually change since it has to keep pace with global constraints and requirements. Universities and planners in education departments have to keep this in mind while framing curriculum and syllabus for different subjects intended to be introduced for prescribed programs. If it is determined to stick to traditional mindset and continues to remain inflexible, nothing will ever change in the system. Students will continue to complain that they don't get options to take a subject of their choice, which would suit their aptitude and also meet their career requirements. And the course content that are being offered may not help them in acquiring the required skills and abilities needed for the career of their choice.

There has always been a mismatch between the demands for vocational skills with the supply of the vocationally trained human resources. The courses offered for vocational education do not seem to be quite in consistence with the skills identified in shortage category, and the shortage skill categories are mostly short-listed in the courses which have been identified.

The following contradictory facts have been revealed in the process of identifying the skills:

> Inadequacy of trained personnel in the shortage skills has continued to be a major hindrance.
> Productions of skills, not in demand, seem to be on the rise.
> Lack of proper identification of courses suitable for vocational skills.
> Lack of a concrete plan investment and employment potentiality.

This has created an enigmatic situation of unemployment among certain categories of skilled workers. It is true that after the inception of the National Technical and Vocational Education and Training program, students' enrolment has considerably increased in the colleges throughout the country. The areas of engineering and business have become the center of attraction for the students and they are selected mainly on the basis of their performance at the school-final examination and the aptitude tests conducted by respective institutions/colleges. Offering of courses are to be determined on the basis of the perception of local needs and the relative demand of the students.

But how much of importance are given to all these important issues, is the question?

Other criteria for poor implementation of all vocational programs are:

- ➤ Unsuitable location of selected colleges/institutions
- ➤ Inadequate staff position
- ➤ Dearth of competent faculty members (in some cases)
- ➤ Inadequate infrastructure facilities
- ➤ Indiscreet selection of courses to be offered
- ➤ Lack of placement facilities

There is a curiously unending contradiction among parents, students and teachers because of the ever-increasing negative notion based on a mistaken assumption about the way today's job market actually works. No doubt there is an increasing positive reaction as well, in respect of certain elements, which are the basic foundation of vocational education i.e., an underlying focus on career preparation, skill-based knowledge, the possibility of challenging careers, attractive pay package and the parent institutes where studied. This line of positive thinking may represent a new trend for the coming generation.

+++++++++++++++++++

III

THE MODALITIES OVER THE YEARS

Vocational training in India is provided on a full time as well as part time basis. Full time programs are generally offered through Industrial Training Institutes (ITIs). The nodal agency for granting the recognition to the I.T.I.s is NCVT which is under the Ministry of Labour, Govt. of India. State technical education boards and some universities offer full time as well as part time courses. Vocational training has been successful in India only in industrial training institutes and that too in engineering trades. There are many private institutes in India which offer courses in vocational education and training, but most of them have not been recognized by the Government.

Various committees and commissions have, time and again, deliberated over the concept of need-based education and essential modalities for the implementation of vocational education. At the beginning of the present century, however, attempts were made to introduce some practical courses like woodwork and drawing in our school curriculum. A little later, practical courses of a vocational nature like metal work, leatherwork, carpentry, tailoring, agriculture, sericulture etc. were introduced in upper primary schools. The objective, however, wasn't to train up students for a vocation but to give their education a vocational bias. Very few students however, opted for these courses. Majority of them opted for Hygiene and Sanskrit.

During the thirties and forties the problem of providing vocational education at the secondary stage became even more important and complicated than ever before due to three specific causes:

o   Increase in enrolment due to the expansion of secondary education. Enrolment was basically not a problem but all who were enrolled didn't have the required interest and aptitude for the so-called literary education of the period. They were rather considered to have the ability to attain a better position through the pursuit of some vocational skills.

o   Increase in the number of secondary schools in rural areas created the problem of adapting these schools to rural needs and environment.

o   Many girls' secondary schools were set up, which posed a real challenge for the founders of such schools and the reason was that devising special courses suited to their requirements at short notice was not an easy task.

The Government of India, therefore, requested His Majesty's Government to send an expert body to India in order to study the problem and make necessary recommendations. In response to the request of the Indian Government, Mrs. Wood and Abbot came to India and after a thorough enquiry, submitted its report on the proper organization of vocational education in India. It was on the basis of this report that in succeeding years, some changes was brought in. The Provincial Governments started technical, commercial or agricultural High Schools and also began to give initiatives in the form of larger grants to private schools providing non-literary courses.

The increasing demand for technically trained recruits during the war and the increasing development of industries paved the way for technical education. Even after the war, the process continued and in the Five-Year Plans of educational reconstruction, an important place was assigned to the provision of non-literary courses at the secondary stage and students had to choose one out of following elective groups:

1. Humanities
2. Science and Mathematics
3. Practical subjects
4. Fine Arts

Practical subjects could more appropriately be called vocational subjects as it included subjects like Agriculture, Carpentry, Electric wiring, Printing, Sericulture etc. These subjects were particularly intended for boys. For girls, Domestic Science, Needlework and Embroidery were introduced.

But the question is: Was real vocational training imparted to the students through these courses?

Perhaps it wasn't. Hence, it was far from being capable of facilitating pupils' direct entry into any related vocation. It is for this reason that admission to these courses was confined to less than 15 percent of the students. The majority of them opted for Humanities and Science and Mathematics, as these subjects had follow-on courses at the college level. This state of affairs continued till the appointment of the Mudaliar Commission in 1952. The two vital recommendations of this Commission were:

- ❖ Introduction of diversified courses at the secondary level.
- ❖ Commencement of multi-purpose schools

Consequently multi-purpose schools were established all over the country consecutively during the fifties with the purpose of training pupils in the best way possible to make them eligible for selected job situations or for higher studies in respective fields. Craft courses of different categories were recommended for making education less literary and more practical as well as instilling in our children the sense of dignity of labour. A quick look at the sequential expansion of Vocational education in the State of Assam will give some idea about the occupational development in this region because it was here that the system of vocational education was first initiated.

VOCATIONAL TRAINING IN ASSAM

The history and present position of technical and vocational education in Assam is perhaps best understood from a review of the circumstances surrounding the establishment and growth of such institutions in other parts of the country. It is observed that states like Punjab, Orissa, Tamilnadu etc hold approximately 79% stake in number of schools which impart vocational training. And Maharashtra is the foremost, holding more than 16%. Schools have an important role in vocational studies because one can start learning a vocation right from his/her school days. More coverage in school with proper infrastructure can create a large technical group in future, which at present is deficient.

India, however, is too large a geographical unit within which this kind of survey can best be undertaken. Few persons are perhaps in a position to make a survey over so wide a field. Discussion at this level is, therefore, mainly confined to conditions prevailing in the province of Assam. However, it can reasonably be said that what is true to Assam is also largely true to most of the remaining provinces of the country.

This should undoubtedly be an essentially fundamental area for comparative study. But at this point of time, I set forth to explore the chronological development of Vocational Training in the State of Assam in Eastern India, the way it expanded under difficult social and material conditions; but which is yet to develop into an important vocational programme.

Chronological Development

Soon after the Second World War, most of the sepoys and non-technical staff working for the British army were released. But as they were rather aged, the British administration thought it prudent to provide them some technical training so that they could earn their livelihood through either wage employment or self-employment. Consequently, a technical training centre named War Technical Institute was instituted at Jorhat with the help of machineries and equipments left behind by the British army. The institute operated successfully till 1947, the year India attained freedom from the British rule.

India was soon after partitioned and a large number of Hindu populace of erstwhile East Bengal driven out of their homes came to Assam as Refugees. This high inflow of refugees was a matter of great concern for the Govt. of India, because most of these uprooted people were either not sufficiently educated or possessed any such skill as to be able to work for a living. With the intention of making these people employable, the Ministry of Relief and Rehabilitation of Government of India decided to arrange vocational / technical training particularly for the youths. Initially, such a training centre was set up at Jorhat, which was followed by one each at Guwahati, Srikona (Silchar) and Nowgong. Technical Education in Assam, however, initially started with the establishment of POW Institute before independence. Establishment of Assam Engineering

Institute and afterwards, Assam Engineering College. was the beginning of Technical Education in the State of Assam. It has been a long journey of evolution of State technical education which is still progressing.

Directorate of Technical Education maintains the government technical and polytechnics institutes in Assam. The courses offered in these centres were both technical as well as vocational in nature, such as:

1. Fitter
2. Turner
3. Welder
4. Carpenter
5. Wireman
6. Motor vehicle mechanic
7. Blacksmith
8. Sheet metal worker
9. Weaving
10. Bleaching and Dying
11. Cutting and Tailoring
12. Electrician

and so on. Till the 1st of April 1956, the Government of India used to bear 100% expenditure for running these training centres and the trades. Thereafter, a new expenditure sharing was agreed upon at the rate of 60% by Govt. of India and 40% by the State of Assam. This continued till 1963 and thereafter the full burden of running the I.T.Is was vested on the Government of Assam.

During the later part of the fifties some private entrepreneurs entered the field of vocational training. They initiated Type Writing and Stenography training courses and also played a leading part in imparting vocational training in Tailoring, Weaving etc. in almost all the major towns of the state. The Govt. neither imposed any control over them nor assisted them in any way whatsoever. But they achieved tremendous success in reaching out to the people and in course of time the motivation was so strong that their employment viability could not be questioned at any quarter. Towards the last part of the sixties, a technical training institute, the first of its kind in the state was established in the private sector at Sivsagar, which also imparted training in technical trades like Fitter, Welder, Carpenter, Blacksmith, Electrician and Wireman. But the Institute died young as the employment opportunities for their alumnus happened to dry up for certain unavoidable reasons.

The Vocational Training was renamed as Craftsmen Training during the sixties and it found a new lease of life with the passing of the Apprentices Act 1961, which made statutory provisions for ex-ITI trainees to undergo apprentice training in industries to obtain certification as skilled technician. The ITI level trained person was graded as semi-skilled technician. The most important development of the period was that the Govt. of India formulated a full-fledged regime for craftsmen training. A Training Manual was prepared accordingly and enforced throughout the country with rigid guidelines for almost all the activities including selection and allotment of land, building construction, financial support and staff pattern etc. Systematic course curriculum was prepared and rigorous training for ITI employees was also arranged.

The Apprentices Act, 1961 was, however, enforced in the state of Assam only in 1965. Prior to that, however, in 1964 the Government of Assam established 5 new ITIs at Barpeta, Bongaigaon, Diphu, Tinsukia and Tezpur. For about five years Tinsukia ITI functioned as a Guest ITI at Jorhat due to ack of proper accommodation at Tinsukia. It shifted to its own premises at Tinsukia in 1970 after the completion of construction of its own building there. Student capacity in the ITIs at Tezpur, Tinsukia and Bongaigaon was 200 plus while for Diphu and Barpeta only 100 seats were allotted. The following trades were to be dealt with in these ITIs: Some of the trades in which these ITIs were expected to provide training have been listed below:

o Blacksmith
o Carpenter
o Cutting and Tailoring
o Draughtsman (Civil)
o Fitter
o Electrician
o Machinist
o Motor Vehicle Mechanic
o Sheet Metal Worker
o Surveyor
o Turner
o Welder
o Wireman   and so on.

Though these trades were technical in letter, they were equally vocational in spirit in the sense that its primary intention was to train a person to a particular vocation. If it is so, then without any ifs and buts it can be assertively said that the vocational education program was introduced in the State of Assam as well along with other states in the sixties. The courses were more or less structured on the pattern suggested by the Union Ministry of Education but study has revealed that the achievement was far below the expected level. The scenario remained the same more or less till 1983, when an ITI exclusively for women was established at Tinsukia in 1985 with financial assistance from North East Council. Some of the areas where training opportunities were provided are —

o Cutting & Tailoring
o Draughtsman ship (Mechanical)

o Embroidery & Needle Works
o Knitting with Machine
o Secretarial Practice
o Stenography

It was in the same year that Assam Gana Parishad came into power as a new local force for the first time. It was appreciable for the new government to take the initiative soon after to increase the number of ITIs by setting up at least one ITI in each district on priority basis. Accordingly, with a paltry additional allocation in the Annual Plan, 11 (eleven) new ITIs were set up simultaneously at Bhergaon, Dhansiri, Dhemaji, Gargaon, Gauripur, Haflong, Karimganj, Kokrajhar, Majuli, Nalbari and one exclusive ITI for women at Guwahati. Most of these ITIs had training facilities for not more than three conventional trades.

A Computer training program named as Data Preparation & Computer Software, the first regular course of its kind was instituted at ITI Guwahati in 1985 with the help and support of the Ministry of Information Technology, Government of India. The same year a single trade ITI was set up at Barama with only Bodo Typewriting in the course, in response to the consistent demand of the Bodo populace of the area. The same course was also introduced simultaneously at Kokrajhar ITI in the same year. But due lack of popularity, the trade was discontinued later on.

In 1986 one unit of DOEACC-'O' Level course was introduced at ITI Srikona with the financial help and support of the Department of Electronics, Government of India.

In 1988-89 the Government of India decided to obtain financial assistance from the World Bank for modernization and up gradation of training infrastructure in all the ITIs throughout the country. The scheme known as World Bank Aided Vocational Training Project came up as a timely support with the following incentives –

- o Supply of modern machineries and equipment
- o Replacement of existing equipments in the ITIs as they were old and obsolete.
- o Introduction of new and modern trades
- o Renovation and repair of old ITI buildings
- o Provision of audio-visual equipments
- o Provision for training of instructors in all ITIs
- o Supply of books for ITI libraries.

11(eleven) Assam ITIs were selected and taken up for up gradation under this project. They are listed below –

1.	Barpeta	7.	Kokrajhar
2.	Bongaigaon	8.	Nalbari
3.	Guwahati	9.	Nowgong
4.	Guwahati (Women)	10.	Srik8. Nalbariona
5.	Haflong	11.	Nalbari
6.	Jorhat		

In addition to other infrastructural support the following new and modern trades were included in the existing syllabus of all the ITIs:

- o Instrument Mechanic (Chem.)
- o Laboratory Assistant (Chem.)
- o Mech. Electronics
- o Mech. Ref. & A/C

Under the same Project three new Women ITIs at Majbat, North Lakhimpur and Silchar were also set up with the following trades –

- o Dress Making
- o Draughtsman (Civil)
- o Hair and Skin Care
- o Mechanic Electronics
- o Secretarial Practice

In 1999 one private ITI was established at Naharkatia, which was subsequently recognized and affiliated to National Council of Vocational Trades, New Delhi. A course specially designed to produce Electricians and Mechanics (Motor Vehicle) was introduced in this ITI.

In the year 2001, during his visit to Shillong, the then Prime Minister of India Shri Atal Behari Vajpayee promised a grant of 100 crores for doubling the number of ITIs in the North Eastern States as well as for up grading the existing ones. As a matter of fact, in accordance with the above declaration a scheme called **PRIME MINISTER'S NORTH EASTERN STATES PACKAGE** was instituted. After thorough discussion with a high level committee with the state, the Government of India decided to implement the scheme in the State of Assam to fulfill the following objectives.

I. Establishment of New ITIs:

1. Dibrugarh   2. Goalpara   3. Hailakandi   4. Morigaon

II. Existing ITIs covered under the Project:

1. Barpeta   2. Bongaigaon   3. Dhansiri   4. Gargaon
5. Gauripur   6. Jorhat   7. Karimganj   8. Kokrajhar
9. Majbat   10. Majuli   11. Nagaon   12. Nalbari
13. Srikona   14. Tezpur   15. Tinsukia   16. Udalguri
17. Dhemaji   18. Dandua   19. Dhubri

III. New Trades introduced:

As discussed above, the following new trades are also introduced phase-wise in different ITIs —

1. Computer Operation & Programming Assistant
2. COPA
3. PPO
4. Electronic Mechanic
5. Draughtsman (Civil)
6. Dress Making
7. Hair and Skin Care
8. Information Technology & Electronic System Maintenance (IT & ESM)
9. Instrument Mechanic (Chem.)
10. Laboratory Assistant
11. Mech. Electronics
12. Mech. Refrigerator & A/C
13. Preservation of Fruits and Vegetables
14. Secretarial Practice

and the government is making all kinds of facilities available to help the institutes provide high-quality training to the trainees so that they become employable in real sense.

IV. Modernization and Supply of Equipments:

New and High-Tech State of Art machineries and equipments were supplied to the ITIs covered under the scheme. For new trade full set of tools and equipments to cope with the prescribed syllabus were also supplied.

V. Civil Works:

17 new buildings and workshops were constructed with immediate effect for the

ITIs which were functioning in rented accommodation since 1985. New workshops were also constructed under the project for new trades introduced in the existing it is.

VI. Training Program for Instructors:

Majority of serving Instructors were deputed for training by the Govt. of India.

Training Institutes were located at the following centres:

1. Chennai, 2. Delhi, 3. Hyderabad, 4. Kanpur, 5. Kolkata, 6. Ludhiana and 7. Mumbai.

VII. Training outside the State for Assam youths:

Youths are deputed from time to time with scholarship outside the state to undergo training in the trades which are not available in Assam ITIs.

VIII. Introduction of Self-Employment Oriented Short-term Courses:

With a view to impart professional skill for establishing self-employment ventures, a special short-term training course of 3 to 6 months duration was designed and implemented in all the ITIs covered under the scheme.

In 2002 **TATA TEA** established an Industrial Training Centre with Computer Operation & Mech.(MV) Trade at Rowta. The ITC was subsequently recognized and affiliated under National Council of Vocational training and it has made abundant progress.

After this, no further projects under government initiation have been undertaken but the above descriptions speak for itself about the tremendous growth and development of vocational education and training in the State during the last fifty years. Notwithstanding the fact that it has developed and expanded under difficult social and material conditions; it is yet to develop into an important vocational programme.

There is no denying the fact that there is tremendous input of trainees in government as well as private institutes in recent times. Better training will definitely increase the demand for ITI qualified people in different trade areas and this will lead to better placement facilities for our youths in the ITIs. After all better education and training means better job opportunities.

Latest trend in the state

In a major reform drive, Education Ministry of Assam, Dr. Himanta Biswa Sarma (2013) declared that vocational education would be introduced in the secondary level within a short span of time – the exact date of initiation was yet to be finalised and announced. The task has been initiated and the preliminary formalities being completed the system will be in operation within the next couple of months.

"This system will be introduced in 100 schools in the State in the next year on an experimental basis", said Dr Sarma. He further said that the students doing the vocational course would be able to get the same evaluation all over the country on the basis of National Vocational Educational Qualification Framework.

From class IX in high schools, the students will be scrutinised to ascertain who will go for conventional education and who will be interested in vocational education. There will be two sections in the class, one of which will be trained with vocational skills along with the textbooks specially prepared for them. The students would have the liberty to continue with the vocational education in the higher secondary and college level or switch over to the conventional education.

Assam Agricultural University has been entrusted to lend a helping hand to prepare the vocational course on subjects like horticulture and pisci-culture. Gauhati University, DibrugarhUniversity and Assam Agricultural University have been entrusted to submit a vision document each as to what these universities would do in the next five years. On the basis of this proposed five-year plan, the State Government would decide to provide financial and other aids to these universities for the development of research works.

Government of Assam has also emphasized on multiple cropping in the state. This definitely necessitates updating of the courses in keeping with the needs and requirements of time and location.

+++++++++++++++++++

Current Scenario of TVET in India

Type of Institutions for Vocational training according to National Sample Survey Organization (NSSO):

The technical education system in India can be broadly classified into three categories –

- Central Government funded institutions,
- State Government/State-funded institutions &
- Self-financed institutions.

Studies conducted by NSSO reveal that vocational training is provided to only about 10% of individuals of 15-29 age-groups. Out of the formal training acquired by that particular age group, only 3% are in a job. Only 20% of formal vocational training is imparted through ITI/ITCs. In India, technical education and vocational training system follows the usual conventional patterns as is followed for the award of bachelors and masters degrees – successful completion of the prescribed courses of study makes the students eligible for diploma from ITIs and polytechnics and certificate level training in it is through formal apprenticeships. Most preferred field of training, nowadays among the youngsters, is computer related training and this training opens the door for both self-employment and wage-employment.

The Vocational Training in India is imparted by mainly two types of bodies:

- Public Industrial Institutes (ITIs)
- Private owned Industrial Training Centres (ITCs)

Some of the principal training schemes are:

- The Craftsmen Training Schemes (CTS)
- Apprenticeship Training Scheme (ATS)

Details about the nature of training and related information are available on the following websites:

- Ministry of Labour (http://labour.nic.in)
- National Council for Vocational Training (NCVT) (http://dget.gov.in)

National Council for Vocational Training is an advisory body set up by the government of India in the year 1956. The Council is chaired by the Minister of Labour, with members from different Central and State Government Departments, Employers and Workers Organizations, Professional and academic Bodies, AICTE, and State Councils for Vocational Training at the State level. It prescribes standards in respect of syllabi, equipment, scales of accommodation, duration of courses and methods of training. It also conducts tests in various trade courses and lays down standards of proficiency required for passing the examination leading to the award of National Trade Certificate and other credentials.

There are two categories of vocational trainings i.e., skill acquisition takes place through these two basic structural streams:

a) Formal and (b) Non-formal.

(a) <u>Formal vocational training</u> follows a well-structured training program and leads to certificates, diplomas or degrees, recognized by State/Central Government, Public Sector and other reputed concerns. Formal sources are government sponsored and hence considered more valid and authentic from the point of employment opportunities in government sectors. The fact that Government may not always be able to provide job facilities to all candidates passing out from these institutes is a different issue. The courses being redundant at times pose problems for job seekers to get placements in private sectors, particularly the reputed ones.

(b) <u>Non-formal vocational training</u> helps in acquiring some money-making proficiency, which enables a person to carry out her/his ancestral trade or occupation. In a way through such non-formal vocational training, a person receives occupational training through 'inherited' sources.

'Non-formal' vocational trainings are also received through 'other sources'. In such cases training received by a person to pursue a trade or occupation, is not hereditary and is different from that of his/her ancestors' occupational pursuits.

A glimpse into the different categories of pioneering Vocational Institutes and the courses which was initially proposed by the Ministry of Education, Government of India, speaks of the diversity that has been attempted while selecting the courses. It becomes clear that course selection has been done after minutely studying the probable requirements for the development of the country's socio-economic status during that period.

INDUSTRIAL TRAINING INSTITUTES (ITIs) AND INDUSTRIAL TRAINING CENTRES (ITCs)

The Directorate General of Employment and Training (DGE&T) in the ministry of labour, Government of India made the first move in 1950 by launching Craftsman Training Scheme CTS and instituting about 50 ITIs for imparting skills in various vocational trades to meet the skilled manpower requirements for technology and industrial growth of the country.

Vocational Training refers to certificate level crafts training and is open to students who are school dropouts and have left school anywhere in between grades VIII and XII. Programme administered under the CTS are controlled and managed by Industrial Training Institutes (ITIs) and Industrial Training Centres (ITCs). This scheme falls within the purview of Directorate General Employment and Training (DGET), under the Ministry of Labour and Employment.

Vocational training in India is provided on a full-time as well as part-time basis. Full-time programs are generally offered through I.T.I.s. The nodal agency for granting the recognition to the I.T.I.s is NCVT, which is under the Ministry of Labour, Govt. of India. Part-time programs are offered through state technical education boards or technical universities who also offer full-time courses. Vocational training has been successful in India only in Industrial Training Institutes and that too in engineering trades. It is only very recently that some other courses have been incorporated in the stream. The vocational training was initially made available in small duration trades such as,

o Electrician,
o Plumber,
o Auto-technician,

o Carpentry,
o Painters,
o Packages,
o Multipurpose Technicians,
o Masons,
o Dairy Assistants, etc.

The following points speak about the task distribution of the training Programmes:-

- The duration of training programme varies from 1-2 years or small duration of 2-3 months.
- The resource persons are generally drawn from engineering departments (rural or otherwise) of state governments, faculty of engineering colleges and polytechnics as well as other ITIs.
- The trainees also require to be provided one or two week's orientation program in relevant industries.
- Training programmes are incorporated in collaboration and financial support of the State and Central Government departments of Science & Technology / Rural Development and Department of Industries as well as funding from business sectors.

POLYTECHNIC EDUCATION

Polytechnic education in India has, to say a truism, contributed a great deal to its economic growth and development. Most of the polytechnics in the country offer three year general diploma courses in the following conventional disciplines --

- Civil Engineering,
- Electrical Engineering and
- Mechanical Engineering.

During the last two decades many polytechnics started offering courses in other disciplines such as

- Electronics,
- Computer Science,
- Medical Lab technology,
- Hospital Engineering,
- Architectural Assistantship etc.

In addition, many single technology institutions are also offering diploma programmes in areas like

- Leather Technology,
- Sugar Technology, and
- Printing Technology etc.

Many diploma programmes are also being offered exclusively for women in Women's Polytechnics, for instance, in –

- Garment Technology,
- Beauty Culture and
- Textile Design.

Polytechnics were basically intended to provide job skills after 10th standard and the duration of diploma courses is 3 years, which means, the trainee becomes employable at the age of 19 years. Post diploma and advanced diploma specialization courses of 1-2 years duration are also offered in some polytechnics.

The aim of polytechnic education is to generate a pool of skill based manpower for the technical and engineering field. The pass-outs of Diploma level Institutions play a significant role in managing operations at different levels i.e., both business and industrial sectors. It is further an accepted fact that small and medium Industry prefer to employ Diploma Holders because of the specific skills they acquire during the course.

In recent years, India has seen a remarkable increase in the number of Degree level Engineering Colleges throughout the country. However, the growth of technical institutions has not been uniform as far as the number of polytechnics and degree engineering colleges is concerned. There is also a common observation that degrees outshine the diplomas in the job market.

A Nation-wide scheme of **"Submission on Polytechnics"** had also been launched. Under this scheme new polytechnic had been proposed for every district, particularly the districts not having a polytechnic already. The existing Government Polytechnics are already in the process of up-gradation and modernization. Efforts are also being made to increase intake capacity by using space, faculty and other facilities in the existing polytechnics in shifts. A shortage of qualified diploma holders has been noticed in several new areas. Therefore, engineering institutions are being upgraded and encouraged to introduce diploma courses to augment intake capacity. Diploma programs could be conducted in evening shifts when the laboratory, workshop, equipment and library are free.

The courses which were initially proposed and sponsored by the Government of India phase-wise for the vocational stream in ITIs and ITCs district-wise in different states are itemized below. The list below also incorporates the courses covered in different areas under Apprentices Act 1961. These courses can be profitably incorporated in all ITIs and ITCs sometimes taking into account local requirements:

Agricultural Sector
- Dairy Farming
- Co-operatives
- Cultivation of Medical Plants and Herbs

- Farm Machines and Engineering
- Fishery / Fish Processing / Inland Fisheries
- Forest Products
- Fruits cultivation
- Vegetable cultivation
- Apiculture
- Floriculture
- Plant Protection / Crops and Management
- Seed Production Technology
- Vegetable Seed Production
- Swine Production
- Horticulture
- Making of Gur (Molasses)
- Oil Seeds/Vegetable Oil Industries
- Pesticides and Fertilizers
- Piggery
- Post-Harvest Technology
- Poultry Farming
- Re-cycling of animal waste
- Rural Construction Technology
- Sericulture
- Sheep Rearing and Wool Production
- Small Farm Management
- Small Processing Units of Paddy, Wheat, Oats, Millets, Bread and Cakes
- Medicinal and Aromatic Plant Industry,
- Sheep and Goat
- Husbandry,
- Repair and Maintenance of Power Driven Farm Machinery,
- Veterinary
- Pharmacist-cum-Artificial Insemination Assistant,
- Agro Based Food Industry (Animal-based),

- Agro-Based Food Industry (Crop-based),
- Agro-Based Food Industry (Feed-based),
- Post Harvest Technology,
- Fish Seed Production,
- Fishing Technology,
- Soil Conservation,
- Crop Cultivation / Production.

Engineering and Technical Vocations

- Air-conditioning and Refrigeration Servicing
- Automobile Servicing and Maintenance
- Boat-Building Practice
- Building Construction and Maintenance Practice
- Cold Storage Maintenance Practice
- Domestic Electronic Equipment Servicing and Maintenance
- Electrical Domestic Appliances – Servicing
- Electrical Equipment Maintenance
- Fabrication Practice
- Field Service Practice
- Foundry Practice
- Furniture Design and Manufacture
- General Mechanic
- Hospital Instrument Servicing and Maintenance
- Industrial Instrument Servicing and Maintenance
- Laboratory Instrument Servicing and Maintenance
- Metal Coating and Painting
- Projection Equipment Maintenance and Repairs
- Quantity Surveying and Specifications
- Television Equipment Maintenance and Repairs
- Watch and Cloak Servicing
- Water Supply and Sanitary Construction
- Civil Construction/Maintenance,

- Mechanical Servicing,
- Audio Visual Technician,
- Maintenance and Repair of Electrical Domestic Appliances,
- Building and Road Construction,
- Building Maintenance,
- Ceramic Technology,
- Computer Technique,
- Rural Engineering Technology,
- Materials Management Technology,
- Rubber Technology,
- Structure and Fabrication Technology,
- Sugar Technology,
- Tanneries

Textile-based Vocations

- Handloom Weaving
- Textile Bleaching, Dyeing and Finishing

Chemical-based Vocations

- Ceramic Pottery
- Cosmetics
- Glass Working
- Leather Goods Manufacture
- Mining
- Paints, Varnishes, Pigments, Lacquer work
- Plastic Molding
- Sports Goods Manufacture
- Soap Manufacturing

Home Science-based Vocations

- Banking
- Designing, Dyeing and Painting

- Dietetics
- Dress Designing and Making
- Food Preservation
- Hostel Management
- Interior Decoration
- Meal Service and Supervision
- Nutrition and Food Preparation
- Textile Designing
- Tie and Dye, Batik Printing and Block Printing
- Toy Making
- Child Care and Nutrition,
- Catering and Restaurant Management,
- Pre-school and Crèche Management,
- Clothing for the Family,
- Health Care and Beauty Culture,
- Bleaching Dyeing and Fabric Painting,
- Knitting Technology,
- Institutional House Keeping.

Humanities Science and Education:

- Library and Information Science,
- Instrumental Music (tabla, drums and other percussion instruments),
- Classical Dance (Kathak etc.),
- Indian Music (Hindustani Vocal Music),
- Photography,
- Commercial Art,
- Physical Education,
- Bharat Natyam,
- Cotton Classifier.
- Pre-Primary Teacher Training
- Primary School Teacher Training
- Physical Education Teacher Training

Diploma Courses in Medical Laboratory Technology

- Ambulance Attendant and Medical Emergency Technician
- BCG technical Assistants
- Dental Hygienist
- Dental Mechanic/technician
- Dietetic Aids
- Diploma in Ophthalmic Technique
- Diploma in Pharmacy
- Dressers
- ECG and Audiometric Technician,
- Junior Medical Social Workers
- Laboratory Assistants
- Medical Record Technicians
- Multi-purpose Health Workers
- Occupational Therapy Technicians
- Operation theatre Assistants
- Orthopedic Technicians
- Physiotherapy Technicians
- Psychiatric Assistants
- Radiological Assistants
- Medical Laboratory / Technology Assistant,
- Health Worker,
- Nursing,
- Health Sanitary Inspector
- Hospital Documentation,
- Hospital Housekeeping,
- Ophthalmic Technology,
- X-ray Technician,
- Physiotherapy and Occupational Therapy,
- Multi-rehabilitation Worker,
- Bio Medical Equipment and Technician,
- Multi Purpose Health Worker,

- Pharmacist,
- Nutrition and Dietetics,
- Auxiliary Nurse and Mid Wives,
- Primary Health Worker.

Commerce and Business Related Courses

- Accounting and Auditing
- Banking
- Book-Keeping and Accountancy
- Commercial Arts
- Data and Key Punching Process
- Insurance
- Internal Trade
- Labour Law Assistants
- Legal Assistants
- Marketing and Salesmanship
- Materials Management
- Office Management and Secretarial Practice
- Radio and Television Processes
- Small Business Management
- Stenography
- Export-Import Practices and Documentation,
- Purchasing and Storekeeping,
- Taxation Practices/Taxation laws/ Tax Assistant,
- Industrial Management,
- Receptionist,
- Basic Financial Services,
- Tourism and Travel,

Miscellaneous Vocations

- Commercial Arts
- Graphic Arts
- Library Assistants

- Museum Assistants
- Photography
- Tourist Guides

Initially, many of these courses were extensively introduced in the vocational institutions throughout the country. Four Regional Colleges of Education were also established phasewise to train up the teachers and adequate funds were invested for the implementation of the recommendations. Schools were entrusted with the task of providing vocational training formally at 10th and 12th levels. It is evident that at the outset, the Ministry of Education had also proposed agriculture-based courses of diverse nature, but very few were introduced in the institutes and the students had little choice.

Soon it became evident that the training imparted in the multi-purpose and vocational schools was not adequate enough to develop the required vocational and technical competence and the students continued to remain as unemployable as before. Consequently, the courses introduced lost its meaning and with the passage of time, the multi-purpose school system started showing signs of heavy losses and absolute collapse. One of the main causes, which need to be mentioned at this point, is that only 25% of the total teaching time was allotted to these courses, and the remaining 75% being set exclusively apart for general education. Further, there wasn't any scope of preferences for the students when they sought admission to Engineering and other Technical institutions. This indeed had a pernicious affect on vocational education. Attempts were made by different bodies to find out a remedy to this alarming situation but no concrete solution could be found until the Kothari Commission (1964-66) made a thorough review of the entire situation and came up with the following recommendations:

- School education should be of 10 years duration.
- It should be general in character and common to all students – no electives.
- Introduction of electives only at the pre-university stage.
- 50 percent high school pass-outs should be diverted to vocational courses at the pre-university stage.
- Vocational education need not necessarily be a 1-year course. It may be of 1-3 years duration depending on the nature and content of the course.
- 20 percent of those who pass Class VII should be diverted to purely vocational courses.
- The rest may opt for general courses without any electives.

The avowed objectives of a progressive type of vocationalisation of education as envisaged by the Education Commission 1964-66 and implemented by the Union Ministry of Education as an integral part of the 10+2+3 pattern of education introduced during that period are:

- ➢ To train persons for middle level jobs particularly in industries and other service sectors.
- ➢ To provide training for self-employment in the field of agriculture, small industries and other allied services
- ➢ To offer vocational courses which are potential by themselves but need not necessarily be highly specialized.
- ➢ To make vocational courses more practical and job-oriented and establish close links between education and employment

It is obvious from these objectives that vocational education intended to provide students the scope to seek gainful employment or get self-employed. It may be noted that apart from alienating the students from general education, the objectives, in its true sense, was to meet the local skill-requirements by training students in the required vocational skills.

In the above context, a very pertinent question that might arise in the mind of every sensible person is:

- To what extent are the objectives really realized?

The answer to this question is hidden in the Pandora box of the mismatch between the courses offered and the skills, which are, as usual, in short supply in the target areas. It is for this reason that the real state of affairs was not satisfactory. Moreover, even the qualification obtained at the end of two-year intensive course was not prized high enough for appointment in government services. Further, there was a widespread assumption that this scheme would prove equally fruitless and unsuccessful as the multi-purpose high school scheme of the fifties and sixties. It can be assumed that this assumption is backed by the false notion that the problem of vocationalisation of education is exclusively an educational problem. But it is rather an economic problem. Vocational courses by themselves cannot create jobs. Jobs will be available and in plenty when economic development takes place. It is then that vocational courses will necessarily be in demand and gain popularity as well. This calls for a massive program of educational and vocational guidance for all categories of students – secondary as well as higher secondary. And to be very frank, there should certainly be an element of compulsion and carefully worked out selection procedures for admission to the different courses as well as in the process of selection of candidates for jobs when they pass out.

Vocationalisation of Education

Vocationalisation of education is expected to bridge the gap between the vocational courses and the requirements of industrialization. Traditional education is too much theoretical and ignores the utility aspects of the courses. It is for this reason that it has tremendously failed to prepare the right products for entry into the employment market.

After passing out secondary or senior-secondary, nearly all students have a very common inclination to go for college education and thereby they waste a couple of years till they realize the futility of pursuing an academic degree incapable of providing them a fruitful employment. If vocational streams were made mandatory at the school level, a good percentage of individuals would not perhaps be lured for college education. Only a small fraction, the academically talented, having an urge to excel in the academic field and become good teachers and administrators would be channelized for University education.

The primary cause of the problem of unemployment being serious in our country is that even in the vast ocean of unemployed people, it becomes difficult to locate the right type of personnel for doing the right jobs. The tragedy is that there is as much surplus of manpower and there is shortage of right personnel.

It goes without saying that in a planned economy, education, beginning with secondary level should be job-oriented. The supply and demand for human resource at different levels should be controlled, directed and regulated by the Government and government regulated bodies. Workforce for specific category of jobs has to be produced to avoid discrepancy in the employment market. Guiding principle for educational planning in any country whatsoever should be: *Right person for the right job'*. All kinds of wastage and destruction involving human and financial resources needs to be checked as it is a great deterrent to the steady economic growth of the country.

It is also apparent that vocationalisation of education will pave the way for dealing with fundamental issues of drop-outs, stagnation and waste, scholastic backwardness etc.

Implications:

1. Vocationalisation is a viable instrument to make career and education go together.

2. Vocatiopnalisation develops motivation as students perceive a correlation between learning in school and world of work requirements.

3. Integration of career education within curriculum becomes more significant and meaningful and not segmented presentations as is reflected in traditional educational programs

4. Vocationalisation provides fresh learning environments and alternative learning strategies, rather unconventional which are needed to deal with the individual needs of students.

5. Vocationalisation provides adaptability, academic skills, job skills, work values, work habits that are needed in the rapidly changing job-related society.

6. Vocationalisation of education develops career skills which includes job hunting skills, decision making skills as well as skills required to retain a job.

7. Vocationalisation tends to interlace education and occupation in the life span of a person.

8. Vocationalisation, can prove very effective in teaching individuals good work habits and positive attitudes towards work.

There was, to say a truism, lack of the required enthusiasm and seriousness in the whole process of implementing these recommendations and the progress of vocationalisation even at the pre-university stage (i.e., after 10 plus) was terribly slow from the very beginning. The Government of India therefore launched a massive centrally sponsored scheme of vocationalization in 1977.

Aims as enlisted in NCERT publication 'Vocational Education' at the +2 stage' (1984):

1. To fulfill the national goals of rural development and the removal of unemployment and distribution.
2. To bring about social transformation.
3. To impart education relevant to productivity, national development and individual prosperity.
4. To meet the need of middle-level manpower for its growing sectors of economy.
5. To divert a sizeable group of students to varied vocational courses.
6. To prevent a mad rush to general education in University.
7. To prepare students for self-reliance and economy.

Keeping these objectives in view, NCERT had initially recommended courses in the following categories i.e.,

a) Language and Literature
b) General Studies [social, political, economic, scientific etc.]
c) Science and Humanities courses designed to understand the basis and scope of various vocation and
d) Social Sciences can be handled well by teachers with a Master's degree in the subject concerned but it should be simultaneously followed by a teacher training program.

Teacher's Role, Status, Service conditions and Education for Teachers are also exclusively devised and projected by NCERT. In respect of vocational subjects involving practical works, it has been mentioned that all teachers should possess basic vocational qualifications and be a master in their respective areas. The service of part-time teachers and instructors like doctors, lawyers and even motor mechanics should be liberally obtained even though they may not have a teacher-training certificate.

Experience, by itself is the best teacher and the involvement of experienced professionals is beneficial in imparting general education but more so in case of skill education. This collaboration would definitely result in a healthy participation, which would be of great help in improving the on-the-job training and employment of the trained personnel. Above everything else it has been suggested that special teacher training or orientation programs for this sector of education should be designed, which would involve not only pedagogic training but also occasional training programs in specific skills and technologies. Part-time staff may be highly qualified professionals but even then for effective classroom instruction, they too would definitely require some amount of orientation in instructional techniques and evaluation. The full-time teachers would require periodical training and re-training to be well informed and equipped with the latest methodologies and practices. But everything in real practice will involve time and money. So a compromise between what is best and need-based would have to be accepted and adopted in the larger interest of this sector of education and the country as a whole. The importance of the preparation of suitable textbooks and related teaching materials has to be taken into account on priority basis keeping in view the need and scope of the subjects offered. The importance of professional education in the present context is well understood. Hence, it would be worthwhile to make a survey of the textbooks that already exists and make essential modifications if required. Necessary steps should also be taken in right earnest to prepare the kind of books needed for the different courses newly introduced.

Soon after, in keeping with the recommendations of NCERT, vocational stream was introduced at the +2 stage in different parts of the country and Assam was no exception. But experience has shown that the courses, which were introduced with great gusto failed to evoke the much-needed response. It was increasingly felt that the courses were intended only for those who were not fit for any of the three streams i.e., Arts, Science or Commerce. Consequently, the government has taken certain initiatives to handle the situation.

Government Initiatives

Keeping in mind that the education system should cater to the needs of the manpower requirement for the fiscal growth of the country, Government of India has accorded high importance to vocational education and training. While elaborating on the essence and role of Education, the National Policy on Education (NPE), 1986 (as modified in 1992) has insinuated that Education builds up manpower for different levels of the economy.

National Policy on Education (NPE)

The NPE 1986 emerged with strongly advocated introduction of systematically planned programs of Career Orientation to Education at the tertiary level.

It observed, **"The introduction of systematic, well-planned and rigorously implemented programmes of vocational**

education is crucial in the proposed educational re-organization."

The implication was that vocational education should be considered a distinct stream, intended to prepare students for distinctly identified occupations spanning several areas of activity. These courses were to be normally provided after the secondary stage but the scheme was to remain open and flexible enough to enable the introduction of these courses soon after Class VIII if necessary. It comprises of certain well spelt out objectives:

- Generating a spirit of initiative and enterprise
- Enhancing individual employability
- Reducing the mismatch between the demand and supply of skilled manpower
- Providing suitable alternative to +2 pass outs
- Restraining them from pursuing higher education without any aim, interest and purpose
- Providing opportunities for the vocational pass outs (+2 levels) to undertake appropriate courses for their career advancement.
- Reducing the gap between the world of work and the world of education
- Linking education to productivity

These objectives seem to have a direct relevance to the policy of progressive vocationalisation of education as recommended by the NEC, 1966. It is also evident that vocational education was intended to be a terminal as well as a transitional course.

- What do we precisely mean by terminal and transitional in this context?

The course is terminal in the sense that students may, if they so desire, take up suitable jobs according to their merits and qualifications after successful completion of the course or get self-employed.

For those, who intend to pursue general education and go for higher studies the +2 course is the transitional course – the gateway to the degree courses.

Vocational Education program was one of the key areas for ensuring logical development of the **Programme of Action** of the **NPE**. The main proposals as envisaged in the programme are enumerated below:

1. State Departments of Vocational Education will introduce vocational programmes for +2 students on experimental basis on a limited scale in different states.

2. Programs at 10+ levels will be formulated by SCERT/SIVEs in the light of guidelines laid down by NCERT.

3. 100 more vocational institutions shall be established to provide more opportunities to students for 10+ vocational courses in Engineering and Technology.

4. A joint Council for Vocational Education (JCVE) will provide stipend in a phased manner to 70% of the higher secondary vocational stream graduates to undergo paid apprentice-ship in appropriate industries.

5. Tertiary level programmes like Diploma in Vocational subjects, Advanced Diploma Programmes and Degree Programmes will be introduced in selected polytechnics, affiliated colleges and universities as well as in special institutes set up for this purpose.

6. Entrepreneur/self-employment skills will be developed in vocational stream students through specially designed curriculum, special training programmes as well as paid apprenticeship facilities.

7. State Departments of Vocational Education and State Councils of Vocational Education (SCVE) will formulate necessary schemes for the purpose.
8. State Directorates of Vocational Education will set up career guidance cells at district level.
9. NCERT/CIVE, SCERTs, RCEs, CDC, TTTIs and other institutes will develop bridge/transfer courses in accordance with the guidelines laid down by JVCE. Suitable schemes for different courses shall be developed by SCVEs.

The policy also recommended health related courses along with other vocational courses based on Agriculture, Marketing, and Social Services etc. at the +2 stage. Tremendous emphasis was given for proper implementation of vocational education as it was considered to play a vital role in developing positive attitudes, knowledge and skills for entrepreneurship and self-employment. The NPE also visualizes the introduction of systematic, well-planned and meticulously structured programmes of vocational education, which can be rigorously carried out to enhance employability, reduce the mismatch between demand and supply of skilled manpower and provide a viable alternative to those undergraduates pursuing tertiary education, without any pre-determined interest or purpose. The policy indicates that efforts will be made to provide children at the higher secondary level with nonspecific (i.e., generic to be more precise) vocational courses which intersect between those which are occupation-specific and which are not occupation-specific.

The National Policy was primarily concerned with the development of a national system of education based on a national curricular framework having a common core along with other components, which may be flexible. The committee for Review of **NPE, 86** envisaged the modalities for a reorientation of content and a systematic process of education. Some of the suggestions provided have been enumerated below:

o The curricula need to be enriched by cultural content
o Value education need to be given priority
o Media and Educational Technology to be employed in all spheres of education
o Work experience to be made an integral part of total teaching-learning process so that this work experience could be carried forward to a higher level of education.
o Teaching of Science and Mathematics to be geared for the true promotion of spirits of enquiry.

Technical Education Quality Improvement Programme (TEQIP)

Government of India has put into operation a Technical Education Quality Improvement

Programme (TEQIP) with the assistance from the World Bank to improve the quality of education and enhance the capabilities of the technical institutions to become vibrant, demand-driven, excellence conscious and competitive at national and international levels. The proposed reforms include

- faculty development,
- examination reforms,
- regular curriculum revision,
- introduction of semester system,
- focus on research and
- Developing awareness for accountability.

National Vocational Qualification Framework

With the purpose of stimulating reforms activities for developing skills and to facilitate nationally acceptable and international comparability of qualifications, a "National Vocational Education Qualification Framework" established by the Central Government. Central Advisory Board of Education (CABE) has resolved to set up an inter-ministerial group which would also include departmental experts and representatives of State Governments so that proper and truly functional guidelines for the proposed Framework can be developed.

The unified system of national qualification, it has been declared, will cover schools, vocational education and training institutions and higher education sector. National Vocational Qualification Framework (NVQF) will be based on nationally recognized occupational standards which would include listing of all major activities that a worker needs to perform to attain competency standards. It will be an exhaustive and detailed listing of the knowledge, skills and attitudes that a worker should possess to perform the assigned task with confidence.

UGC's initiative: A positive step

With a view to making the first-degree courses veritably relevant and meaningful to human life and to the developmental needs of the country, the UGC, during the Fifth Plan, initiated the scheme of restructuring of courses at the undergraduate level. The University Grants Commission has well-formulated scheme of Career Orientation to Education with well-designed Career Oriented Courses. The objective of the scheme is to ensure that the graduates who pass out after completing these courses are awarded Certificates, diplomas and advanced diplomas and are expected to be well-equipped with all the necessary knowledge, skills and aptitudes for gainful employment in relevant job sectors. There are also a lot of prospects for self employment.

The programme was proposed to comprise four major components:

1. Foundation courses
2. Core courses
3. Selected applied studies
4. Involvement in national or social service programmes for the first two years

In spite of sufficient amount of money being invested in the programme, the scheme could not make much progress. But yet the UGC took another bold step forward and launched the Scheme of Career Orientation to Education at the first-degree level in 1994-95 in conformity with the NPE 1986 updated in 1992. A committee was subsequently appointed to look into the feasibility of its introduction. It identified the important courses to be introduced and listed out as many as 58 subjects which would help our students become more readily employable as well as provide them the much needed skill and ability to grab self-employment opportunities. It has been repeatedly emphasized that identification and implementation of the right type of vocational courses is indispensable for enhancing individual employability and building up the students as self-employed and independent citizens. But the overall progress of vocationalisation and its effective linking with the basic socio-economic needs of the people at the tertiary level is dismal and depressing.

Higher Education in India, on the other hand, has been treading on the same path since 1957 i.e., the year of its inception. Time has changed – there is already a tremendous development in the field of science and technology. But there is hardly any change in the form or structure of the curricula for different subjects in many universities. It is for this reason that students have increasingly lost confidence in higher education institutions for preparing them to fit in the job market. The chief employer of the educated youth in this country, even today, is the State, which simply does not look beyond academic certifications. It is only recently that requirement like NET (National Eligibility Test) and other pre-determined criteria have been fixed for appointment of lecturers in colleges and universities.

The UGC has given accordance to the introduction of value-added job-oriented diploma programs in colleges and universities. It has come up with clear-cut instructions that colleges should supplement its degree courses with certificates/ diplomas/advanced diploma programs to equip all graduates with necessary skills so that they become better employable in the increasingly competitive job market. The UGC management has even offered a special financial grant to selected colleges for every life-skill course introduced. This may work as a powerful incentive for those financially poor and under graded colleges that are interested in upgrading their status for the better. Expert committees have been constituted to study and facilitate revision of college and university syllabuses at least once in five years to cope with changing demands of job requirements. Though lately, importance of skill-based job-oriented courses has been realized and the issue has become a crucial theme for all the conferences and seminars in higher education. And the new mantra that has become the basis of every recent discussions and debates related to education is *'Make every graduate and post-graduate employable'*.

The XII 5-Year Plan has tried to carry forward the task envisaged by the Eleventh plan to undertake a vital project of launching a National Skill Development Mission that may bring some changes in 'Skill Development' programmes and other initiatives. The State governments are supposed to be entrusted with the task of engaging some of their Departments or Agencies for constituting a State Skill Development Mission. Some selected private sector bodies can also play vital roles as the private arms of the Mission.

Proposal forwarded by the National Skill Development Policy 2009

1. A range of national qualification levels – based on criteria with respect to responsibility, complexity of activities, and transferability of competencies;
2. Certification for learning, achievement and qualification;
3. Comparability of general educational qualifications and vocational qualifications at appropriate levels;
4. Competency based qualifications and certification on the basis of nationally agreed standards and criteria;
5. Different learning pathways – academic and vocational – that integrate formal and non-formal learning, notably learning in the workplace, and that offer vertical mobility from vocational to academic learning;
6. Guidance for individuals in their choice of training and career planning;
7. Lifelong learning through an improved skill recognition system; recognition of prior learning whether in formal, non-formal or informal arrangements;
8. Modular character where achievement can be made in small steps and accumulated for gaining recognizable qualifications;

9. Multiple certification agencies/institutions will be encouraged within NVQF.

10. Nationally agreed framework of affiliation and accreditation of institutions;

11. Open and flexible system which will permit competent individuals to accumulate their knowledge and skill through testing & certification and qualify for higher diploma and degree;

12. Quality Assurance regime that would promote the portability of skills and labour market mobility;

13. Quality Assurance regime that would promote the portability of skills and labour market mobility.

14. The avoidance of duplication and overlapping of qualifications while assuring the inclusion of all training needs;

The Mission to be operative under Prime Minister's National Council on Skill Development for apex level policy directions and National Skill Development Co-ordination Board constitutes the following:

A. Prime Minister's National Council on Skill Development – National Council headed by the Prime Minister as Chairman.

B. National Skill Development Co-ordination Board – The board headed by the Deputy Chairman of the Planning Commission. It will act as a non-profit company under the Company's Act with appropriate governance structures, Board of Directors being drawn from outstanding professionals and experts.

C. The National Commission for Enterprises in the Unorganized Sector (NCEUS) – It has been set up as an advisory body for the informal sector to bring about necessary expansion and development in the productivity of these enterprises and for generating large scale employment opportunities on a sustainable basis, particularly in rural areas.

D. Public Private Partnership (PPP) – Major emphasis had been given on the PPP mode for the first time in the Eleventh Five Year Plan. It primarily focuses on:

o Private Investment in Skill Training

o National Framework for domain specific standards and common principles

o National database for the establishment of location-wise availability and shortage of skilled personnel

o Providing options of multiple entry and exit points and total mobility between vocational, general and technical streams

o Special emphasis on economically weaker sections

o Overcoming the regional disparities caused by diverse socio-economic factors

The Twelfth Five-Year Plan also envisaged making the proposed Apex Skill Development Institute a full-fledged arrangement – a reality so that it can proceed with the task of taking initiatives on program testing, certification, curriculum setting, faculty development, introduction of new elective courses in IITs/ IIMs. **Apex HiTech Institute, Bangalore**, commonly known as AHI, Bangalore has been accordingly set up by the Directorate General of Employment and Training (DGE&T), Ministry of Labour and Employment, under **Government of India** in the year **1993.** It is one amongst the pioneer Institutes of national interest in skill development initiatives.

Initiatives to be taken up at the State Govt. level during the 12th 5-year Plan comprise of the following:

o Modernisation of Employment Exchanges, which will act as career counseling centres.
o Modernisation of existing ITIs
o Giving more autonomy to educational institutes.
o Execution of PPP mode
o Personal policy to ensure accountability and productivity

Main focus of the Eleventh as well as Twelfth 5-year Plan is to organize a joint collaboration between the States and the Centre and also to give a boost to private partnerships to create an estimated 58.6 million new jobs in the domestic economy and about 45 million jobs in the international economy. World Bank also has taken initiative through its Millennium Development Goal to impart training and education in India.

Recent Developments

The latest development in India is the premeditated and much awaited declaration of the government that vocational education will be introduced at the secondary school level from Class IX. The move is a part of the national drive to provide vocational training to 550 million students by 2022.

Revision of the scheme of "Vocationalisation of Higher Secondary Education".

Centrally Sponsored Scheme of "Vocationalisation of Higher Secondary Education" has been revised and now it is known as **"Vocationalisation of Secondary and Higher Secondary Education"**. The Scheme has already been included under the Rashtriya Madhyamik Shiksha Abhiyan scheme with effect from 1st April, 2013.

The major modifications in the latest scheme are as follows:-

i) Introduction of Vocational Education from **Class IX** onwards i.e. at the secondary stage.

ii) **75:25** sharing pattern between Center and States for funds released under all the components of the scheme. **90:10** sharing pattern for funds released to the North Eastern States including Sikkim.

iii) Provision for a flexible pool of **Rs. 14.50 lakhs** per annum per school for engaging resource persons including Teachers/Skill Knowledge Providers/ Trainers etc.

iv) Provision of financial costs for engaging with the Industry/Sector Skill Councils (SSCs) for assessment, certification and training.

v) Enhancement of funds for purchase of books and e-learning material.

vi) Financial provision (**1%** of total budgetary outlay) for Innovative Programmes under vocational education.

vii) Cost of development of curriculum and learning materials to be a maximum of **Rs. 2.00 lakhs** per skill level per job role.

viii) Performance linked incentive to Govt. aided and recognized, unaided private schools.

Higher and Technical Education Ministry has also announced setting up vocational universities in all the states. Besides it is supposed to have on the cards a special policy on vocational education. As a step forward, the government has already taken the proposal to set up an unusually exceptional committee for recommendations on various projects for vocational education in the country.

The committee has been assigned certain significant responsibilities such as

- setting up <u>Vocational University</u> where post-graduate <u>vocational</u> courses can be taught. It will also look after graduate and even under-graduate courses.
- reviewing the present syllabus of vocational courses at Class XI and XII level,
- providing lateral and vertical mobility to students of vocational courses,
- recommending ways of accreditation for vocational courses and
- introducing vocational courses at secondary school level.

To do away with the alarmingly increasing dropout rates, it is considered necessary to give occupational training to the students that will provide them employment opportunities and make them self employable.

The World Bank Report 2006 (Skill Development in India, The Vocational Education and Training System) has specified that employers prefer students with general education skill in addition to vocational skills. Therefore, to make students more market worthy, curriculum in <u>schools</u> or institutions providing vocational education and training must emphasize on equipping students with general academic skills which may include the following fundamental skills:

- problem solving,
- analyzing,
- business development and
- marketing skills.

The vital need of the hour is to take immediate steps to establish adequate number of Vocational Universities with industry participation. With independent universities, students will get the opportunity to undergo undergraduate and graduate courses that are required and designed by industries. The present vocational courses can be affiliated to universities and special emphasis given on industry relevant job skills training with strong back-up of modern technology. This can be the most preferred choice to enhance the significance and value of the courses. Experts say that employees in all job sectors must strive hard to enhance their employability for personal growth and universities can help ensure that one has all the relevant skills required in a specific job area.

+++++++++++++++++++

IV

BASICS FOR SUSTAINABLE TVET

General Education and vocational education have a lot to contribute to the whole education system. There should be proper co-ordination between these two spheres of education keeping in view the modern trend of avoiding multiple streams at the school level. If the course offered is seemingly doubtful in respect of career advancement and future prospect of the students, it would definitely be unwise to compel a student to opt for that course or subject. Just as a singer who has a large repertoire of songs to perform wins the heart of the audience, a comprehensive system of school education ambivalent in character and content, i.e., a combination of general academic subjects as well as vocational subjects, can only provide a healthy learning experience for the students. This scheme of education is increasingly being adopted in U.K., U.S.A., Japan and other developed countries for the simple reason that it tends to promote employability and has proved to be immensely useful in life.

It is an undeniable fact that an emerging economy as it is; India today has the need of a huge workforce, skilled and well-trained, to pick up the pace of increasing socio-economic growth. Skill shortage is evident in every sector in this country. In sharp contrast with the economies of the developed countries, where burden of an ageing population is pulling down their growth rates, India has over 550 million people who are 25 years or younger. However, to say a truism, herein lies the paradox. While we have huge potentials in terms of young generation, we have an equally colossal shortage of skilled people in almost every sector. This talent deficit has tremendously impeded growth in the manufacturing and service sectors. Education system in our country has incredibly failed to support the rising demand for skill sets. As already stated above, there is also a big question mark on the employability of students who receive higher education.

Studies conducted and published by the World Economic Forum (WEF) have revealed that only 25 percent of Indian professionals are considered employable by organized sector. They have specifically mentioned that there is an urgent need for higher quality vocational education to train and equip our youths in a better way for jobs. We need graduates who have the confidence to get involved, who think critically about their work, and who have the initiative to find ways of doing things better.

Having acknowledged the seriousness of this fact, the government has done a commendable job by coming to a decision for setting up the National Skills Commission and National Skills Development Council for a rapid and revolutionized change in the system.

It is true that with this initiation an ecosystem has been created, but it will take time to evolve any substantial configuration as such. National Skill Development Policy has disclosed that the current capacity of skill development programmes is just 3.1 million, against the ambitious target of India to make skill-based training available to 500 million people by 2022.

In India, National Skill Development Corporation India (NSDC) is one of its kinds which promote Public Private Partnerships. It aims to promote skill development by catalyzing creation of vocational institutions with excellent features. And of course, this creation is possible only when we have highly competent and dedicated human resource in management and teaching.

NATIONAL POLICY ON SKILL DEVELOPMENT

A National Policy on Skill Development has been formulated by the Ministry of Labour & Employment with the purpose of generating a workforce, well-resourced with adequate knowledge and globally acknowledged credentials. Only a work-force well-equipped with enhanced skills and aptitudes can gain admittance to decent employment and ensure India's viability in the vibrant Global employment market. The policy proposes to increase the productivity of workforce in various sectors, where increased participation of youth energizes the process for national development and prosperity. Well-designed skill development schemes can sustain employment generation, economic growth and social development process and become an integral part of comprehensive economic and social policies and programmes. A framework for better coordination between various stakeholders i.e., Ministries, States, Industry etc. has to be ascertained, which will promote excellence and meet up the requirements of knowledge economy.

Mission

National Skill Development Initiative, well-implemented, can give power and ability to all individuals through enhanced skills, knowledge, and aptitudes. This quality will facilitate easy access to decent employment and guarantee India's competitiveness in the global market.

Aims

The aim of National Skill Development is to sustain the obvious inevitability of achieving rapid and inclusive growth by way of:

- Enhancing individuals' employability and ability to adapt to changing technologies and employment market demands.
- Improving efficiency and productivity which will upgrade the living standards of the people.
- Strengthening competitiveness of the country.
- Focusing on investment in skill development.

Objectives

The key objectives of the National Policy on Skill Development are to:

- Create opportunities for all to acquire skills throughout life, and especially for youth, women and disadvantaged groups.
- Endorse commitment by all stakeholders to be the owner of skill development initiatives.
- Build up a high-quality skilled workforce/ entrepreneur competent to cope with current and emerging employment market needs.
- Enable the establishment of flexible delivery mechanisms that act in response to the uniqueness of a wide range of needs of stakeholders.
- Facilitate effective coordination between different ministries, the centre and the states and public and private providers.

Scope

The range of the National Policy on Skill Development includes the following:

- Institution-based skill development including ITIs/ITCs/Vocational schools/technical schools / polytechnics/ professional colleges etc.
- Learning initiatives of sector-wise skill development organized by different ministries and departments.
- Formal and informal apprenticeships and other types of training enterprises.
- Training for self employment/entrepreneurial development.
- Adult learning, retraining of retired or retiring employees as well as lifelong learning
- Non-formal training including training by civic society organizations.
- E-learning, web-based learning and distance learning.

Essential Prerogatives

The urgent need of the hour is to redefine the critical elements of imparting vocational education and skills training in proper perspective and making them flexible but significantly pertinent, all-encompassing as well as innovative and resourceful enough to address the contemporary need of the country.

The skills to made available in TVET have to be familiar with:

- New business requirements;
- Need to improve quality of education and trainings at all levels; and
- Need to make technical / vocational education system more flexible and inclusive for sustainable growth.

And the need is embossed in the maxim – '**Better Job skills, better prospects**'.

Three questions which need to be initially looked into are:

What is a skill?

What are job skills?

What are the essential prerogatives for a right job?

What things is a person good at doing?

Skill is the ability to do something competently and well.

Skills are the activities that a person does proficiently and well.

All of us are gifted with several skills. Sometimes it is difficult to recognize the skills that you have. But a skilled person has enough ability, experience and knowledge to be able to do something well.

Job skills are abilities a person needs for a particular job. For example, a cobbler needs to know how to repair shoes. A doctor whose job is to treat people who are ill needs to be well-trained in **Medical Science**. A teacher, whose job is teaching, needs to be well-equipped in the **Methodologies of Teaching**. A taxi driver needs to know how to **drive a car** and **read traffic signs and signals**. <u>A Computer system analyst</u> must be able to communicate with the users of his system, and be able to listen to them to find out their requirements. He must be able to **investigate** and **solve problems**.

Skills may be transferable as well as non-transferable. Transferable skills are skills we can use in different jobs. We can obtain skills from one job and utilize them in a very different job. Speaking English well, for instance, is a skill we can use in almost any kind of job. Some examples of transferable skills are teaching other people, solving problems, accepting responsibility, organizing projects, making decisions, and creating new ideas. Employers want to select people who have already acquired the skills or who have the ability to learn the skills necessary to do a particular job within a time frame.

The personal skills required in different jobs are surprisingly similar, with just a few differences in the level of skill required. Every profession demands you to have good **VERBAL** and **WRITTEN COMMUNICATION** skills, and we also need to have the ability to **CO-OPERATE** with other people. Employers will assess these skills at every stage of our application. So, one has to be very careful while preparing the resume.

BASIC ESSENTIALS FOR THE RIGHT JOB

As the emerging market base is expanding at a very fast pace, it opens up new options of opportunities and in the process it speaks of a distinct role to contribute for the professionals, the domino effect of which is the new revolution of employment prospects. Therefore, professionals need to be ready to crave their position in order to face the competition powered by intellectual stratagem to occupy their space as per the requirements of career dimensions of the organization. Employment is efficiency followed by competence to mark our pathway in the job market that defines our career cycle at a potentially prospective periphery. Priority, therefore, needs to be given to developing the following skills as a precondition to gain entry into any kind of profession.

a) **Communication skills:**

This is one of important tool for getting suitable opportunities. The ability to express ideas clearly and confidently in speech and in writing is vitally essential in business or any other job sector. Distinct and clear expression is something that helps the employer to know about ourselves and our experiences. It is the device to convey what we are trying to do in our life and thereby prompt the Organization to take a correct decision for our profiles — whether to offer the job or not. The art of communication or the ability to share his thoughts and ideas clearly is what an individual needs to develop from the very beginning of his career planning. Today, most institutions including the corporate houses give maximum credence to it, and a vocational graduate or diploma holder with good communication skills can't but be the preferred choice of all employers.

A course on **COMMUNICATIVE SKILLS AND PERSONALITY DEVELOPMENT**, if integrated with the vocational degree programs will act as a bonus for all skilled professionals. Good communication skills enable a person to put across his point correctly. For example, when someone is sent to a customer for 'requirements analysis', initially he has to find out the customer's needs and then report it back. For this, good oral and written communication skills are important. But only <u>an ELT professional with attractive personality and a good background of Phonetics and Spoken English will be the best choice for conducting a course of this standard. A certificate or diploma on Personality Development may be considered essential in specific cases. To be frank others may not be squarely dependable for this job.</u>

b) <u>Body Language:</u>

It involves presentation skills which is considered a vitally essential component in all job sectors, particularly the corporate world. It defines the right kind of attitude, which indirectly speaks about us and our personality and also about all our characteristics as a distinct individual. It is the nucleus of any job options and is clearly manifested right at the interview table. Professionals need to build all those qualities based on their natural excellence, competences and calmness that defines their authenticity in the edge of competitive world, which clearly indicates who we are and where we stand; and it is this which is going to act in accordance with the expectations of the employers in any organization.

This is entirely a core aspect for an individual based on his/ her qualification and according to that their application process for the right profile that they have applied. Technical aspects must analyze deliverables and skill set as per the domain needs and requirements of the Organization in terms of selecting the right candidature for the right options. It is this aspect which explains about future performances in the job market at a reflective and adequately reasonable parameter.

c) **Technical skills:**

This is entirely a core aspect for an individual based on his/ her qualification and according to that their application process for the right profile that they have applied. Technical aspects must analyze deliverables and skill set as per the domain needs and requirements of the Organization in terms of selecting the right candidature for the right options. It is this aspect which explains about future performances in the job market at a reflective and adequately reasonable parameter.

d) **Relationship Management Skill:**

It is one vital skill that an individual needs to develop from the very beginning of their career life cycle. Professionals need to take best possible advantage of networking sites – For example, Linkedin.com, Face book, Twitter and so on, to get in touch with their seniors and Alumni, and also with the professionals who also belong to the same professions or Industry. Apart, from that they can also be in touch with several Industry experts when they are in the campus. They should make it a prerogative to attend seminars and conferences for professional growth and use e-mails to express their ideas about Organization growth potential aspects would, in the long run, go a long way in building the healthy relationship for totality of career growth and advancement.

e) **Life Skills**:

Life skills are behaviors used appropriately and conscientiously in the management of personal affairs. They are a set of human abilities acquired through education or direct experience that are used to handle problems and issues commonly encountered in daily human life. Life Skills have been defined as all the non-academic foundational skills human beings learn and use to thrive individually and live optimally in community with others. They are abilities for adaptive and positive behaviour that will enable individuals to deal effectively with the demands and challenges of everyday life. Studies have revealed that individuals who develop these skills in a positive, rather than preventive manner, feel a greater sense of competence, usefulness, power, and belonging whatever organization they belong to.

f) **Study Skills:**

Study skills are approaches applied to learning. They are generally considered essential for acquiring good grades to be able to get good placements, and useful for learning throughout one's life. There are a range of study skills, which may tackle the process of organizing and taking in new information, retaining information, or dealing with appraisals. To be more precise, any skill which enhances a person's ability to study and pass exams with credit can be termed a study skill, and this includes time management and motivational techniques as well. Study skills are distinct practices that can be learned, usually in a short time, and which can be applied to almost every field of study. They are, therefore, required to be distinguished from approaches and stratagems that are specific to a particular field of study e.g. art, music or technology, and from abilities inherent in the student, such as aspects of intelligence or learning styles.

g) Qualification/ Education:

Education in its universal sense is a form of knowledge acquisition in which the knowledge, skills and habits of a group of people are transferred from one generation to the next through teaching, training, or research. Education normally takes place under the guidance of others, but may also be self-directed. Any experience that has a formative effect on the way one thinks, feels, or acts may be considered educational. Self-directed learning can be more authentic when it is primarily based on formal skill-based education. Every individual needs to build their primary impression on the employers and also to give an idea about their appraisal of the Institution that they belonged to. And our performance in the interview communicates to the board some idea about the education background and the degree acquired. So, professionals need to identify the right institution and obtain proper qualification that explicates the value of their educational attainments. It is this which directs the path to a right kind of job options in the employment scenario at large and puts across their technical and non-technical aspects which reflect the right code of behavior for the right domain.

h) Literacy:

Literacy is the ability to read for knowledge and interest, write coherently, and think critically. Literacy encompasses a complex set of abilities to understand and use the dominant symbol systems of a culture for personal and community development. These abilities vary in different social and cultural contexts according to need, demand and education and it is no less important to be able to get employed and retain the job for a lifetime. Literacy thereby involves a gamut of learning in enabling potential individuals to achieve their goals, to develop their knowledge and potential, and to participate fully in the employment market.

i) **Organizing**:

Organizing is the function employed to achieve the overall goals of the organization. This skill deals with the ability to design, plan, organize, and implement projects and tasks effectively within an allotted timeframe. It also involves goal-setting. What we need today is a results-driven achiever with exemplary planning and organizational skills, along with a high degree of detail orientation. A true achiever will have the ability to decide what steps are needed to achieve particular goals and then implement these.

Organization harmonizes the individual goals of the employees with overall objectives of the firm. The entire philosophy of organization is centered on the concepts of specialization and division of work. The division of work is assigning responsibility for each organizational component to a specific individual or the concerned group. Individuals form a group and the groups form an organization. Thus, organization is the composition of individual and groups. Individuals are grouped into departments and their work is coordinated and directed towards organizational goals. To make optimal use of resources such as men, material, money, machine and method (the 5Ms), it is necessary to design and run the organization properly. Work should be divided and right people should be given right jobs to reduce any possible wastage of resources. As important is the ability to organize, so is the ability to carry out the assigned responsibilities. People should be well qualified and properly trained for both categories of jobs.

What do Employers actually want?

Every employer would be looking for a specific set of skills from job-seekers that match the skills necessary to perform a particular job. But beyond these job-specific technical skills, certain skills are nearly universally sought after by employers. It is the unique combination of skills and values that every employer would be looking for in his employees. The good news is that most job-seekers of today possess these skills to some extent. The better news is that job-seekers with weaknesses in these areas can improve their skills through training, professional development, or obtaining coaching/ mentoring from someone who understands these skills.

The best news is that once we understand the skills and characteristics that most employer seek, we can tailor your job-search communication — our resume, cover letter, and interview language — to showcase how well our background aligns with common employer requirements.

Numerous studies have identified these critical employability skills, which are frequently referred to as "soft skills." Attempt has been made to distill the skills from these many studies into this list of skills most frequently mentioned. Sample verbiage describing each skill has also been included; job-seekers can adapt this verbiage to their own resumes, cover letters, and interview talking points.

Most sought after Skills

Based on a number of intensive surveys on the skills required by technical and other graduates undertaken by **Microsoft** and other organizations, In addition to the skills mentioned above, here is a brief summary of some more skills which were most often deemed important and these are the **skills that present-day employers demand of job-seekers**. Some of these skills might look 'not worth mentioning' but they are the essence of employability.

Analyzing and Investing Skills

These are a set of essential skills to develop the ability to gather information systematically to establish facts and principles. It also entails the ability and self-confidence for problem solving i.e., the ability to review difficult situations, seek multiple perspectives, gather additional information if necessary, and identify key issues that need to be addressed. It requires highly analytical thinking with demonstrated talent for identifying, scrutinizing, improving, and streamlining complex work processes. It is the ability to debate and argue a case interpreting complex material; picking out inconsistencies in reasoning as well as analyzing data from an experiment.

Computing Skills

Almost all jobs today require some basic understanding of computer hardware and software, especially word processing, spreadsheets, and email. Everywhere the need of the hour is Computer-literate performers with extensive software proficiency covering wide variety of applications. Employers today look for candidates with a good knowledge of word-processing, using databases, spreadsheets, the Internet and email, designing web pages etc. A computer literate can definitely rule the day in the employment market today.

Flexibility/Adaptability/Managing Multiple Priorities

The ability to manage multiple assignments and tasks, set priorities, and adapt successfully to changing conditions and environments. One needs to be a flexible team player who thrives in environments requiring ability to effectively prioritize and juggle multiple concurrent projects.

Interpersonal Abilities/ Interpersonal Sensitivity

The ability to relate to co-workers, inspire others to participate, and take the edge off all conflicts with co-workers is essential, given the amount of time spent at work each day. One needs to be a proven relationship-builder with unsurpassed interpersonal skills to be successful in life. He recognizes and respects different perspectives and is open to the ideas and views of others.

Leadership/Management Skills

While there is some debate about whether leadership is something people are born with, these skills deal with our ability to motivate, take charge and direct others i.e., the ability to manage our co-workers. A goal-driven leader maintains a productive climate and confidently motivates, mobilizes, and trains and equips employees to meet high performance standards.

Multi-cultural Se.nsitivity/Awareness

Diversity is possibly the biggest issue in the workplace, and job-seekers must demonstrate a sensitivity and awareness to other people and cultures. A true professional has strengths to include cultural sensitivity and an ability to build rapport with a diverse workforce in multicultural settings.

Decision Making

A competent professional can confidently and boldly determine the best course of action. He can analyze and evaluate options based on logic and fact and come up with instant solutions.

Developing Professionalism

A sincere and honest employee pays care and attention to quality in all his works. He is a true professional because he does not hesitate to support and give power to others.

Problem-Solving/Reasoning/Creativity

This skill involves the ability to find solutions to problems using creativity, reasoning, and past experiences along with the available information and resources. He needs to be an innovative problem-solver who can generate workable solutions and resolve complaints to the satisfaction of all concerned.

Teamwork Skills

There are countless jobs involving group-works, today's job-seeker must have the ability to work confidently with others within a group in a professional manner. Because he is programmed to achieve a common goal, he should be a resourceful team player who excels at building trusting relationships with clients and colleagues.

Commercial Awareness

Commercial awareness skill insists on understanding business predicaments and realities affecting the organization.

Self-Awareness

One should have tremendous awareness of achievements, abilities, values, aptitudes and weaknesses and what he or she wants out of life. It is only then that they can move forward in life with confidence and success.

<u>Time Management</u>

This skill involves the ability to prioritize tasks and manage time effectively. It also emphasizes on developing the capability to work within deadlines.

<u>Numeracy</u>

It entails the importance of being good in calculations. The ability to multiply and divide accurately, calculate percentages, use statistics and calculator, interpret graphs and tables makes a person really employable.

<u>Creativity</u>

Creativity refers to the intrinsic quality of a person having the power to do something on his own, something which requires not merely mechanical skill but intelligence and imagination. A creative professional has the ability to generate and apply new ideas and solutions.

<u>Independence</u>

It speaks of the instinctive freedom to be able to accept responsibility for views and actions and to work under their own direction and initiative.

Two other skills which are also considered important by employers are:

- <u>Global Skills</u>: A proficient employee has also the ability to speak and understand other languages. He /She should have an intrinsic aspiration, to openly show appreciation for other cultures and traditions.
- <u>Negotiating and Persuading</u>: The person should also have tremendous ability to influence and convince others, to discuss and arrive at agreements. Such an employee can't but be an asset for any organization.

Other Essential values

Of equal importance, in addition to the apparently professed critical skills are the moral values, personality traits, and personal characteristics that employers hunt for. One has to look for ways to interlace paradigm of these characteristics into his resume, cover letters, and answers to interview questions. But most of all, these qualities are to be imbibed in the person himself to be able to maintain dignity in the profession over the period of one's working life.

1. <u>Honesty and Integrity</u>

Employers, in all probability, respect personal integrity more than any other value, especially in view of many recent corporate scandals. They are usually on the lookout for seasoned professionals whose honesty and integrity provide for effective leadership and optimal business relationships. Such a professional adheres to standards and procedures, maintains confidentiality and has the guts to question inappropriate behaviour.

2. <u>Adaptability and Flexibility</u>

This category deals with openness to new ideas and concepts, to working independently or as part of a team, and to carrying out multiple tasks or projects. The employee needs to be highly adaptable, mobile, positive, resilient, patient risk-taker who is open to new thoughts and ideas.

3. <u>Dedication/Hard-Working/Work Ethic/Tenacity</u>

Employers seek job-seekers who love what they do and will keep at it until they solve the problems and get the job done. It is only possible when he is a productive worker with solid work ethic who exerts optimal effort in successfully completing the tasks in hand.

4. <u>Stress Tolerance</u>

Employers value persons who can continue to maintain effective performance even under pressure

5. <u>Drive</u>

Employers are always on the lookout for someone who has the determination to get things done. A sincere worker persists in making things happen and constantly keeps looking for better ways of doing things.

6. <u>Dependability/Reliability/Responsibility</u>

There's no question that all employers want employees to report for work every day on time. They also look for people who are ever ready to work and who have the guts to take responsibility for their actions, who are dependable and sincerely committed to excellence and success.

7. <u>Loyalty</u>

Employers want employees who will have a strong devotion to the company — even at times, when it is felt that the company is not necessarily loyal to its employees or is not doing justice to them. Employers are on the lookout for loyal and dedicated manager with an excellent work record.

8. <u>Positive Attitude/Motivation/Energy/Passion.</u>

The job-seekers who get hired and the employees who get promoted are the ones with drive and passion; and who demonstrate this enthusiasm through their words and actions. They are energetic performers consistently cited for unbridled passion for work, sunny disposition, and upbeat, positive attitudes.

9. <u>Professionalism</u>

Professionalism deals with acting in a responsible and fair manner in all our personal and work activities, which is seen as a sign of maturity and self-confidence. It demands being highly organized, dedicated, and committed to one's own occupation.

10. <u>Personal Impact / Self-Confidence</u>

Let's understand it this way: if we are a unique mixture of skills, education, and abilities and don't believe in ourselves, why should a prospective employer trust us? We should be confident in ourselves and what we can offer to the employers. Employers will definitely be in search of a confident, hard-working employee who is committed to achieving excellence and has the ability to present a strong, professional, positive image to others which inspires confidence and commands respect.

11. <u>Initiative / Self-Motivation</u>

While teamwork is always mentioned as an important skill, so is the ability to work independently, with minimal supervision. Highly motivated self-starter takes initiative with minimal supervision and gets things done. He has the ability to act on demand and in critical situations, identify opportunities and proactive in putting forward ideas and solutions.

12. <u>Willingness to Learn / Lifelong Learning</u>

No matter what our age is, no matter how much experience we have, we should always be willing to learn new skills and techniques. Jobs are constantly changing and evolving, and we must show an openness to grow and learn with that change. Employer values a job-seeker who is enthusiastic, knowledge-hungry learner, eager to meet challenges and quickly assimilate new concepts. One who continues to learn throughout life develops the competencies needed for current & future roles.

Skill-based Education — the Pathway to Employability

A bird's eye view on the major limitations of the existing education system manifests that it has apparently failed to give due importance to vocational education and skill development. It is this which is primarily responsible for the existing mismatch between the demand and supply of skilled manpower resulting in increasing deterioration in all manufacturing and service sectors today. Every year we churn out millions of graduates and diploma holders, who do not possess the specific skill sets required to become competent professionals in their respective domain. If this trend continues, it will pathetically upset our economic growth prospects in near future. Planners should reflect on making vocational education obligatory in school curriculum without any further delay. In India, we are more preoccupied with the motive of acquiring a degree rather than opting for vocational education and making ourselves more employable and productive. This has created a situation where we see scores of unemployed graduates on the one hand and on the other tremendous shortage of skilled workers in every sector throughout the nook and corner of the country.

It is to be appreciated that the government has finally acknowledged the inevitable need of technical and vocational education for the growth and prosperity of the country in real perspective and a lot of good work has already started to boost up this venture. Partnering with private organizations is vitally essential to obtain necessary knowledge and techniques to build requisite infrastructure and attain the required proficiency to bridge the present gap. However, it would be an extremely arduous task to attain this unless creating necessary capacity building for skill development and trained faculty becomes a reality. And it is one of the most difficult and critical task to be realized in Indian context. Equally, the inability of many universities and institutes to design shorter and affordable curriculum that will get them the required job at a competitive remuneration is another major challenge for the country. The equation of expenditure and degree of excellence is imperative to ensure that the agenda is met to the satisfaction of all concerned.

These are some of the major challenges to be met. But equally important is the judicious use of technology, well-structured curriculum as well as the mode of delivery. These issues, if properly met, can only resolve the expenditure and quality question to a great extent. We can also look for guidance and help, if necessary, from the models of other developed countries where vocational training has become a boon for growth and progress in almost every sector. At present, vocational education is offered primarily at +2 stages in our country and since the system does not have the required scope for vertical mobility, whatever skills are obtained by the students happens to get forgotten and lost at a very short interval.

Only a skill-oriented and broad-based system of education backed by multi-option strategies has the potential to acquaint students with the required academic knowledge and information in different fields of activity to make them potentially employable in the present job market. However uniformly organized the education system may be, without a vocationally viable component within it, it is as disintegrated system of education as can be, totally unethical and out of tune with the thinking and practice of the twenty-first century.

It is for this reason that most of the degree programs offered in academic colleges continue to be traditional and fail to equip the graduates to opt for a definite and successful career. They pass B.A. / B.Sc. and seem to be at doldrums as to what to do next. One feels that their three years of college education was a sheer wastage of a huge bulk of human resource. Hence, there is an urgent need to revert to re-engineering education. Re-engineering is a management term that calls for throwing out everything that is not functional (not in keeping with the modern requirements) and recommends reconstituting a workable system on the basis of completely fresh ideas. Business processes have been in recent times meticulously re-engineered for bringing efficiency, effectiveness and economy. This has become possible because of the unprecedented development in the field of communication and information technologies.

The nature and scope of occupations has become wide and varied. It has tremendously changed with rapid developments in science and technology but curricula have practically remained as it was fifty years ago. The principal employer of the educated youth in India is still the State, which doesn't virtually look beyond academic certifications i.e., graduates, post-graduates etc. for selection of candidates for employment. It is only recently that the system has received a bolt with strict instructions from UGC, NCTE, AICTE and NAAC for specific norms to be followed in determining eligibility criteria. Strict adherence to the given norms may bring about certain changes in the job sector centering round colleges and universities, notwithstanding the fact that good marks in examinations cannot always be sensible criteria for an effective classroom teacher. The hard reality is that majority of employment opportunities today are in the private sector and this sector is indeed very selective and it looks for candidates who possess the required skills and competencies for a particular job. Its requirements are continually changing for the simple reason that this sector has to keep a constant pace with its global competitors. Education therefore, has to be tailor-made to the requirements of the private sector. It is in this context that the need for new courses and course combinations has been felt for meeting varying learning needs of the students for a dependable career. Vocational orientation to education should enable the youth to acquire the requisite skills, techniques and knowledge to become more employable and useful for the nation. Definitely, it will go a long way in reducing the mismatch between the demand and supply of skilled manpower leading to unprecedented economic growth and national development. All pre-degree and degree programs need to be made skill-based. Barring a few recently introduced programs like Computer Science, Hotel Management, Biotechnology etc. restructured on UGC-recommended lines in some of the affiliated colleges, the coverage of these courses is still limited. Introduction of the courses mentioned above may not incur heavy financial involvement on the part of the government either, since they can be operated with the barest minimum core faculty members, three at the most. It is the subject experts and experienced professionals in different capacities that have to be paid for their service. There has always been an underlying feeling among all sensible thinkers that other important disciplines also could be introduced without the least variation in the structure of the existing faculty members or too much financial involvement in the modification and alteration of the infrastructure facilities. An attempt has been made in this document to analyze certain socially desirable objectives, which have to be realized for proper implementation of courses having maximum job opportunities. Some strategies and justification for the introduction of the new Skill-based / Craft-based degree programs have also been outlined for a better comprehension of the whole issue. It is expected that proper implementation of the suggested strategies will go a long way in achieving far-reaching changes in the field of technical and vocational education by opening new avenues and challenging opportunities for all those who persevere and burn the midnight oil and pass with credit.

GESTALT VIEW ON SOME SKILL-BASED SUBJECTS

Vocational education, as afore said, comprises of a number of courses and skill-based subjects. Some fresh skill-based subjects are newly introduced in many private institutes and some government institutes and Engineering colleges. These subjects of diverse nature which can be considered relevant in respect of generating more lucrative and challenging employment opportunities are listed below for ready reference:

A. Subjects related to earth sciences and mining –

- o Applied Geology
- o Petrochemical / Oil Technology
- o Surveying and Drilling Exploration
- o Soil Engineering
- o Seismology and so on.

B. Subjects related to Health Sciences –

- o Microbiology
- o Immunology
- o Enzyme Technology
- o Dental Hygiene
- o Medical Transcription
- o Diet and Nutrition
- o Fitness Management
- o Message Therapy
- o Yoga Therapy and so on.

C. Power Sector [Non-conventional sources of energy] –

- o Solar Energy
- o Wind Power
- o Hydro-power

A potentially viable area for the new generation can be a degree in **Renewable Energy**. India has abundant wealth of renewable energy – abundant sunshine, breezy coastlines and fast flowing rivers. If properly harnessed, it would be possible to provide sufficient electricity to most of our rural belts. It is unfortunate that, in spite of huge potentiality of renewable resources, the country currently produces only around 14,000 megawatts of renewable energy when its total installed power generating capacity, according to the Union Ministry of non-conventional energy sources is around 1,50,000 MW. The reason why a resourceful country like India is not able to use the renewable energy resources in its totality is lack of properly trained and skilled manpower.

In any of the non-conventional energy fields, extensive research is necessary to develop new technologies which will be cost effective and reliable. But professionals are needed not only for research but also for the industry. With companies like Suzlon, Moser Baer, TATA BP Solar, Wipro Eco-Energy, Reliance and others investing in the non-conventional energy sectors, it means a lot of jobs will be available for the qualified and deserving candidates, who also can go in for innovative projects as part-time activity in related field of interest.

A. Service Sector –

- o Advertising
- o Business Management
- o Business Communications
- o Entrepreneurship

- o Hoarding and Storing (Storage)
- o Journalism and Mass Communication
- o Logistics
- o Marketing and Management
- o Marketing and Salesmanship
- o Mass Media
- o Media Consultancy
- o Multimedia
- o Personnel Management
- o Print Media
- o Public Relations and Media Management
- o Telecommunication
- o Trading and Distribution
- o Transportation and Communication and so on

Some other relevant disciplines having implicit employment and production value and which have tremendously fascinated today's generation are:

- · Aromatherapy
- · Bar Management
- · Career Counseling
- · Civil Construction
- · Communicative English and Personality Development
- · Corporate Secretary ship
- · Disaster Management
- · Dyeing and Printing
- · Ecology and Environment
- · Event management
- · Family Counseling
- · Fashion Designing
- · Film / TV serial editing
- · Furniture and Wood Work Construction
- · Garment Production and Export Management

- Gem and Jewelry Designing
- Hair and Beauty Therapy
- Human Rights Education
- Make-up and Skin Treatments
- Peace Education
- Personal Grooming
- Plastic Goods Manufacturing
- Psychology and management
- Psychotherapy and Counseling
- Textile Technology
- Voice acting and so on.

It would be worthwhile to reiterate that these varied programs of diverse nature can be offered at the undergraduate level. The concerned departments may initiate with a Certificate Program. Advanced Certificate and Diploma Programs may be introduced phase-wise so that those who wish to improve their career may opt for such courses after the successful completion of the Certificate course. Certificate program may be a one-year intensive course but Advanced Certificate and Diploma programs should necessarily be a course of 2-3 years duration depending on the availability of proper infrastructure facilities and qualitatively competent faculty. These programs will definitely go a long way in assuring a path to useful employment for the students. Programs should, however, be designed carefully and need to be frequently updated to cover all aspects of education in this field, thus catering to global demands.

Some subjects for the Certificate program at this stage may be —

- Apparel and Fashion Technology
- Applied Sciences
- Automobile Engineering

- Biomedical Engineering
- Biotechnology
- Civil Engineering
- Computer Science and Engineering
- Computer Technology
- Electrical and Electronics Engineering
- Electrical and Electronics Engineering
- Electronics and Communication Engineering
- Fashion Technology
- Information Technology
- Instrumentation and Control Engineering
- Mechanical Engineering
- Metallurgical Engineering
- Production Engineering
- Textile Technology and so on.

The higher level courses can be formulated and designed to meet a higher level of demand in the respective job areas. Some such courses can be —

- Applied Electronics
- Automotive Engineering
- Biotechnology
- Communication Systems
- Computer Integrated Manufacturing
- Computer Science and Engineering
- Control Systems
- Embedded and Real Time Systems
- Energy Engineering
- Engineering Design
- Industrial Engineering
- Industrial Metallurgy
- Information Technology
- Infrastructure Engineering

- Lean Manufacturing
- Power Electronics and Drives
- Product Design and Commerce
- Production Engineering
- Software Engineering
- Structural Engineering
- Textile Technology
- VLSI Design and so on.

The syllabi should be carefully framed to cater to the needs of the industry sector and future requirements.

Some of the **Advanced Topics and Electives in related field** are:

- Aerodynamics of Road Vehicles
- Alternate Fuels
- Automotive Instrumentation
- Automatic Transmissions
- Automotive Instrumentation
- Automatic Transmissions
- Automotive Instrumentation
- Computational Fluid Dynamics
- Design for manufacture and assembly
- Modelling and Simulation of Internal Combustion Engines
- Two and Three Wheelers
- Special VehiclesTwo and Three Wheelers
- Unconventional Engines and Hybrid Vehicles
- Vehicle Maintenance and Testing and so on.

Innovative Projects and research works:

Students with scientific temperament and having mathematical skill and aptitude can go for research-oriented projects in subjects like:

- Applied Chemistry
- Applied Mathematics
- Applied Physics
- Computer Science and Technology
- Materials Science and so on.

Projects involving some amount of research work in related field will open doors for more research and higher studies in related field in future. Well thought-out innovative projects in each of the above categories might open doors for superbly breathtaking innovations and ground-breaking discoveries. Students can also be involved to actively participate in the following categories of innovative projects in automotive segment:

- Design, Manufacture and Testing of different categories of 2 wheelers
- Design, Manufacture and Testing of all Electric Vehicles – vehicles of the future
- Remote Controlled 1:10 scale Cars propelled with IC engines with Methanol as fuel
- Hybrid vehicle development (3 wheelers and 4 wheelers)
- Performance and emissions testing of Bio-diesel produced from animal fats (chicken, for example)
- Simulation of new developments in Fuel Cell using CFD
- Design, manufacture and testing of Composite usage for Bumper, Crankshaft, Propeller Shaft and Valves
- Aerodynamic Simulation of a road vehicle using CFD

These are just a few projects to consider. There may be many more depending on the availability of resources.

<u>Production Courses</u> in the following category can prove a very innovative and challenging activity for the students:

- Internal Combustion Engines
- Manufacture of Automobile Components
- Production Technology

The department should be well-equipped with laboratories like —

o Automotive System Simulation Lab
o Embedded Systems Lab.
o Engine Testing and Trouble Shooting Laboratory
o Sensors and control laboratory
o Vehicle Design Lab,
o Vehicle Servicing Laboratory,

This will go a long way in providing the students with a basic knowledge of mechanical engineering courses and specialization in the following Core automotive Courses thus making them highly trained to meet the needs of the automotive sector:

Core Automotive Courses

- Automotive Electronics and Electrical Systems
- Automotive Emissions and NVH
- Automotive Ergonomics and Vehicle Body Analysis
- Automotive Transmissions and Motor Vehicle Engineering
- Design of Engine and Auto Components
- Internal Combustion Engines
- Vehicle Component Design
- Vehicle Dynamics

The automotive manufacturing sector has been growing at a faster pace than the automotive sector because of the excellent competence of Indian engineers and keeping this in mind, some important courses in Production Engineering can very well be included, depending on the availability of proper infrastructure and competent faculty.

The faculty of respective departments should go in for unceasing pursuit to get technical papers published in various National and International conferences and journals.

Agriculture-based courses:

A proper analysis of the socio-economic data like population, occupation, availability of land resource, cropping pattern, natural resources, industries etc. might be helpful in identifying certain valuable rural-based disciplines, which if properly designed and implemented, might prove instrumental in bringing about a tremendous change in the economic growth and development of the rural sector leading to an unprecedented improvement in the quality of life. Programs specifically for this area can be:

- Agriculture and Plantation Management
- Animal Farming
- Apiculture
- Cotton cultivation
- Cultivation of cereals, pulses etc. and Processing
- Cultivation of sugarcane and Sugar Technology
- Dairy Farming
- Fishery
- Floriculture
- Forest and Wildlife Management
- Horticulture
- Leather industry
- Poultry Farming
- Soil Conservation and Water Management

Many of these courses are already introduced in ITIs and a good many multi-purpose schools but as time passed not much success could be noticed. It is essential to update the course management and some new trades can be introduced in schools as well as colleges depending on the needs and requirements of the locality. With proper thinking and planning two to three courses can be smoothly conducted in a college without too much extra financial burden on the institution. In fact each industrial unit should by itself be an incentive for the vocational institutions within its vicinity to open a related course for the benefit of its students.

Paramedical Courses:

Paramedical courses are one of the principal sources of vocational trained persons in the field of medical industry in recent times. Paramedical Science primarily deals with emergency medical cases and Medical Colleges where aspirants are groomed to administer life-saving medical aid to patients suffering from a trauma are called paramedical colleges. Paramedical courses are distinctively known for their effective involvement in training paramedical personnel to take care of people's life particularly in rural sectors. In general, an aspirant opts for courses like anatomy, toxicology, first aid and drug administration. But the door is open for all kinds of wide-ranging subjects which are in great demand today. Some of these subjects are enlisted below:-

Paramedical Diploma Programs with Specializations:-

1. Diploma in Medical Lab Technology (DMLT)
2. Diploma in Ophthalmic Technology (DOT)
3. Diploma in Radiography Technology (DRT)
4. Diploma in Operation Theatre Technology (DOTT)
5. Diploma in ECG Technology (DECG)
6. PG Diploma in Geriatric Medicine (PGDGM)
7. PG Diploma in maternal and Child Health (PGDMCH)

8. PG Diploma in Drug Regulatory Affairs (PGDDRA)
9. Diploma in Neuro Technology (DNT)
10. Diploma in Dialysis Technology (DDT)
11. Diploma in Dental Hygienist (DDH)
12. Diploma in Dental Mechanics (DDM)
13. Diploma in Endoscopic Technology (DET)
14. Diploma in Dental Operating Room Assistance (DDORA)
15. Diploma in Pharmacy (D. Pharm)
16. Diploma in Health Inspector (DHI)
17. Diploma in ENT (DENT)
18. Diploma in Pathology (DCP)
19. Diploma in General Nursing and Midwifery (DGNM)
20. Diploma in Auxiliary Nursing and Midwifery (DANM)
21. Diploma in Medical Imaging Technology (DMIT)
22. Diploma in Renal Dialysis Technology (DRDT)
23. Diploma in Anesthesia Technology (DAT) And so on.

Paramedical Bachelors and Masters Programmmes:-

1. Bachelor of Medical Lab Technology (BMLT)
2. Masters in Medical Lab Technology (MMLT)
3. Bachelor of Optometry and Ophthalmic Technology (BOOT)
4. Masters of Optometry and Ophthalmic Technology (MOOT)
5. Bachelor of Radiation Technology (BRT)
6. Masters of Radiation Technology (MRT)
7. Bachelor of Occupational Therapy (BOT)
8. Masters of Occupational Therapy (MOT)4
9. Bachelor of Physiotherapy (MPT)
10. Masters of Physiotherapy (MPT)
11. Bachelor of Medicine and Bachelor of Surgery (MBBS)
12. Bachelor of Pharmacy (B. Pharm)

13. B.Sc. (Basic Nursing)
14. Master of Pharmacy (M. Pharm)
15. MD (Physiology)
16. MS (General Surgery)
17. MD (Paedriatics)
18. MS (Orthopaedics)
19. MS (Opthalmology)
20. MD in (Doctor of Medicine)
21. MD (Dermatology)
22. MD (Medicine)
23. MD (Microbiology)
24. MD (Pharmacology)
25. MS (Anatomy)
26. MS (ENT)
27. MS (Surgery)
28. MD (Community Medicine)

And so on.

An accredited paramedical school or college offers hoards of paramedical courses and candidates encounter with a given choice of varied range of subjects. But unfortunately even today there are very few proficient professionals compared to the large size of the rural population. We also need to seriously focus on the availability of proficient Radiographers, Pharmacists and Laboratory Technicians to be a strong support in medical service for rural India.

Looking a little further beyond what has been traditionally designed, implemented and accepted will prove helpful in bringing about the desired change; and the system can then be said to be truly destined to bring about development and prosperity in all fields of activity.

Industries play a significant role in generating employment, which is the base for the economic development of any nation.

Definitely, the need of the hour is to introduce certain courses linked with different types of industries. Industries with employment and production value have to be identified and courses designed in that direction, so that university products in the target areas may be able to find employment or get self-employed i.e., start their own business units. Potentially viable units can be Agro-Animal Husbandry based, Forestry based, Mineral based, Renewable energy sector and so on. And in all these sectors, we need technicians from vocational/technical institutes and colleges. Our country is rich in forest and mineral resources and there are abundant opportunities for more forest and mineral based industries. Even for the proper growth and development of the existing industries there is always a constant demand for skilled and trained manpower. Therefore, the colleges adjacent to such units may introduce courses on related fields, which will have immediate employment opportunities for its students. Facilities for practical training can be obtained from the industrial units in the vicinity. Renewable energy sector has a distinctly different identification of its own. Almost all renewable energy courses are postgraduate courses and since it is an emerging field, it should be a wise choice for many. Both science and technical graduates can join this field, and therefore, apart from energy professionals, students from the Indian Technical Institutes (ITIs) can be in demand for maintenance and other technical jobs. There are short-term diploma programs for anybody interested in the clean energies. If we want India to lead in the clean energies, we need to fix our dreams and go ahead for a degree or diploma in the field. If such courses are not available locally, interested candidates can log in at

- www.cwet.tn.nic.in;
- www.speri.org;
- www.wbreda.org;

- www.mithradham.org;
- www.aaidu.org and also
- www.teriuniversity.ac.in for all diploma and other short term courses in this field.

For postgraduate degrees at a later stage, however, we may log on to:

- www.tezu.emet.in
- www.lkouniv.ac.in
- www.jadavpur.edu
- www.pmu.edu and also
- www.teriuniversity.ac.in

Bio-informatics and related fields

Information Technology decade has witnessed Indian entrepreneurial spirits soaring sky high with the rise of the dot. com wave leading to every kind of research and development in different fields, which has paved the way for the emergence of many a new combinations. One of the most important fields, for example, is the science of Bio-informatics. Three one-year diploma programs are being conducted at the Bio-informatics Institute of India. They are:

1. **Bio-informatics:** It involves the application of IT to the management of biological information. Prospective employers are Pharmaceutical companies in India and abroad, R&D organizations, Universities and other Institutes where similar courses are taught, government institutions, software companies and product marketing companies. There are also immense avenues open for those who intend to work as scientists, software developers, database developers, consultants, trainers, academicians and researchers in related fields.

2. **Chemo-informatics:** It involves a wonderful combination of chemistry and computation and is the management of data, information and knowledge of chemical compounds and their measured properties. Placement is now available in agro- business, chemical and pharmaceutical companies in India and abroad.

3. **Biomedical Informatics:** It involves the application of IT in all domains of health sciences. Placement scope is rapidly increasing in such areas like health care and hospital management systems, laboratory automation, quality control departments, financial management and resource allocation, health services and biomedical research, retrieval and database management systems, health education, research and support systems etc.

Some new universities and institutes have also come up with courses in Bio-informatics, but without proper guidance and counseling as well as the capacity of the institutions to cater to the demand of placement requirements, nothing much can be expected merely from the introduction of the courses.

There are hundreds of courses to begin with but the need of the hour is to provide ample scope of flexibility in selecting a course of one's choice. And of course, proper guidance and counseling is essential.

Introduction of skilled-based courses may not incur heavy financial involvement on the part of the government either, since they can be operated with the barest minimum core faculty members — three at the most. It is the subject experts and experienced professionals in different capacities that have to be paid for their service. The expenditure to be incurred in developing the curriculum and designing and preparing the study materials is to be silently borne by every conscious government in spite of the financial crisis that it might be burdened with due to unwanted wastage and loss of human and financial resources under difficult circumstances. Committed team of professionals in different departments will ever be on their toes to help and work for the government, provided the government shows the urge to do something for the cause of human resource and the nation. Human resource is, after all, the backbone of the nation.

++++++++++++++++++++

V

PROBLEMS & CHALLENGES

Vocational training has been successful in India only in industrial training institutes and that too in engineering trades. At present diverse courses are taught in different schools, colleges and Institutes throughout the country. There are many private institutes in India which offer courses in vocational training and finishing, but most of them have not been recognized by the Government. But it is not known how and why certain institutions, which have limited infrastructure facilities and dearth of competent teachers, and therefore do not, in realistic terms, cater to the needs and aspirations of the students were selected for vocational courses. It is an undeniable fact that the Directorate of Vocational Education in Assam as in many other states miserably failed to follow definite criteria for permitting schools and colleges to start these courses. It is expected that the Directorates in different regions should have made a careful investigations of every necessary aspect and concentrated on the following criteria before granting permission to start vocational courses:

- The need of vocationally trained personnel in respective areas.
- The availability of necessary academic infrastructure.
- Proper survey and identification of the location.

- Fund allocation and strict regulation for timely release of funds.
- Instruction for proper utilization of fund and its timely report to the directorate.
- Provision for additional remuneration for additional works for principals and headmasters as well as faculty members, which will work as an incentive for more work and better work.

It cannot be said that the Directorates had not considered these points; but may be it failed to strictly follow the criteria for reasons beyond its control as it usually happens in Indian context. Situations might have hustled it into a hasty decision in starting the courses, which in another way, was responsible for a second situation in which institutes without the minimum basic academic facilities were permitted to offer vocational courses. As a result of which, in course of time many schools and colleges, particularly the Higher Secondary Multi-Purpose schools were compelled to close down the courses. Despite incessant efforts made at the initial stage to popularize these courses, several problems prevented even the ITIs/ITCs from reaching common masses and youth.

It is therefore considered appropriate to identify the problems and highlight the prospects on priority basis in the light of increasing demand for some of the vocational courses, which have, with the change of time, started gaining ground more as professional courses rather than purely vocational.

Problem Areas identified

Problem areas have been located and identified as decisively crucial in respect of the prevailing Technical and Vocational Education and Training System in India:

1. In our country there is a high dropout rate at Secondary level though the situation is a little different in Assam, Mizoram, Kerala and some other states. Large parts of the 18-24 years age group are never able to reach college. Compared to countries with similar income levels it has been found that India does not under perform in primary education as such but has a comparative deficit in secondary education. But state variations are there and we get a slightly different picture in some states, Assam being one of them.

2. Vocational Education is presently offered at 10 plus stage. But it is also a fact that most students reaching this level prefer to go for higher education. Since the present system does not allow vertical mobility, knowledge and skills obtained seem to get lost. Enrollment in eleventh and twelfth standard of vocational education in our country is only about 4-6% of students at post secondary level. Studies have revealed that students enrolled in vocational education schemes tend to comprise of only about 40% of the available student capacity in these schools.

3. Global scenario suggests that employers mostly want young workers with strong basic academic talent and aptitude and not just vocational skills. The present traditional system of education does not put much emphasis on general academic talent but on written examination results.

4. Healthy participation is lacking. There are no incentives for private entrepreneurs to be involved in the field of technical and vocational education.

5. Present regulations are very inflexible. In-Service training is vitally essential for proper growth and improvement of the workers as well as the organization

but it is limited and not as useful as it needs to be. There is no follow-up action after a particular set of training and hence training programs, however intensive, provide little opportunity for continuous skill up-gradation and there is total loss of money, material and resources.

6. Academically qualified teachers are there but there is dearth of experienced and competent teachers to train students on vocational skills. In foreign countries it is obligatory for all teachers to have at least Bachelors of Vocational Education (BVE) with specialization. However, in India there is no such regulation for the purpose of imparting specific qualifications for Vocational Education teachers.

7. Vocationalization at all levels has not been successful. Training being qualitatively poor is not in keeping with industry needs.

8. Mobility is not well defined and hence there is no definite and clear path for vocational students to move from one level to another.

9. Till date there is no clear policy or system of technical and vocational education leading to certification/ degrees presently available for the unorganized/ informal sector. No Credit System has been formulated for the same. Over 90% of employment in India is in the Informal sector. None of the programs have been rigorously assessed and evaluated. There seems to be utter confusion all through.

10. Expansion of vocational sector is slowly taking place and policies have been formulated to introduce technical and vocational education right from the secondary level but consideration for placement problems and possibilities should be given priorities rather than giving priorities merely on the schedules.

11. Employers still experience problems finding employees with the right skills. In most cases, these shortages are evident in trades that are offered by the ITIs/ITCs – implying that their students do not go well with employers' needs. Most employers feel that ITI graduates do not perform well enough in the use of computers, practical use of machines, communications and team work practices. Employers also feel that graduates lack practical knowledge and need significant on-the-job training to upgrade their skill levels to match the needs of the industry.

The First Move — Initial problems

It is clear that instituting a specific course in a selected school or an Industrial Training Institute demands the fulfillment of certain pre-determined criteria. It is nature and quality of the institute, which determines the value and utility of a particular course. But we cannot ignore some basic things, which are equally important in this respect. They are:

- Proper survey, identification and numerical estimate of skills that are on demand in a particular locality where a particular course is to be started.
- Proper study of the resource capacity and competence of target schools, colleges or industrial institutes.
- Matching of local demand for specific skills and skilled personnel with the available facilities of the institution.
- Identification of skill shortages in the selected areas.
- Proper selection of trained and skilled personnel for the courses and subjects selected.

It is an undeniable fact that no sincere attempt was made for a substantial period of time, to properly estimate the demand for the required skills in respective areas; and whatever attempts were made failed because it was beyond the resource capacity and competence of the target institutes to make proper estimates. It is also true that the Directorates in different regions tried to sponsor surveys at the district level; but the surveys didn't yield any result in respect of fulfilling the requisite criteria. Based on the survey conducted, the situation can be assessed for determining the courses to be introduced in a particular locality. In Assam, for example, a guiding factor in the selection of courses can be – 'to what extent the silk worms can be produced here'. This again needs two things – silkworm raisers as well as skilled and experienced inspectors and examiners. Similarly we have to be guided by the growth of textile industry in the vicinity if we intend to introduce the Textile Technology course in schools and colleges. But on earlier occasions, in different places, of course not everywhere, the authorized principals and headmasters applied a type of trial-and-error method, where the procedure followed was to make an announcement of the course and response from the students was invited, which was then assessed and analyzed. If the responses were encouraging, the course was retained; else it was instantly dropped. These methods were more or less crude in form and unreliable for a proper estimation of the demand for vocational skills. But due to lack of required statistical data and a prescribed norm, the principals were left with no alternative but to follow the trial and-error type of methods. So everything was a matter of guesswork and not something derived from proper deduction and hypothesis. But with experience it was established that any future expansion of vocational courses would not be possible without a reliable estimates of the demand for vocational skills. Now who will take up the responsibility of identifying skill shortages in selected areas is the question. Then only we can think in terms of appropriate strategies for proper estimation of the demand of these skills.

Lack of Basic Infrastructure facilities

Successful teaching of any course or subject depends on the availability of adequate infrastructure facilities in appropriate form. Vocational course can be no exception. Everybody is more or less aware of the types of infrastructure that are required for proper functioning of a school or college. It is the perception of infrastructure that forms the positive attitude of an institution. Of the three latent perceptions of infrastructure facilities i.e., basic, supportive and activity-based, the vital one is the manpower i.e., the teaching staff. Under the present conditions, separate teaching members are recruited in vocational institutes for every additional course, that too, on ad hoc basis. Very often they are appointed part timers and part timers have their own problems and obligations. They are locally available professionals having practical knowledge in their field of work. Basically self-employed technicians are expected to have a better technical know-how and can guide the students in a better way than fresh graduates, who lack the experience as well as practical orientation required for teaching vocational courses. But for an employed person, if not deputed by the department or government for a particular assignment, obtaining permission of his superiors becomes a tiring affair. This is a never-ending common problem, which sometimes ends in turmoil for both the seniors and the juniors.

A circular to this effect from the Government to all private and public institutions, with necessary instructions to encourage their employees or subordinates or juniors to take up part-time teaching of vocational courses as and when approached, may bring about a tremendous change in the whole system. Further, as for a fresher he should preferably be well-trained and oriented in his subject prior to his appointment in any technical or vocational institute. Experience and re-orientation will make him a better teacher. In government schools and colleges as well as in industrial training institutes (ITIs) sometimes due to erratic procedures, there is unnecessary delay in the allocation and release of grants, which tells heavily on the proper growth and development of the institution. There are occasions when the teachers are seriously concerned about job security due to irregular payment of salary and non-incentive workloads. If this happens there can be no productive work and the institution suffers. This is indeed a very serious matter. Further, if the job is not of a permanent nature and a fresher is appointed on an ad-hoc basis and the remuneration is fixed with no other incentive, there is every probability that the situation will be still worse. Administrative lapses and delays may possibly be taken care of, what is difficult to tackle is the changing nature of the teaching jobs – the non-permanent or the semi-permanent jobs.

Lack of standard textbooks

It is true that technical and vocational courses are expected to depend more on practical work but textbooks have their own importance in every course. It is due to lack of standard textbooks that vocational courses in India have failed to make much progress. Teachers may not directly complain but the hard fact is that they are obliged to consult books prepared by foreign authors, which to say a truism, may not quite suit to our conditions. Courses thus suffer due to lack of good textbooks. But again, where textbooks are available, it has been observed that teachers are not competent enough to handle them because the books are written in English and most teachers working in those institutions have poor comprehension ability in the language. Accountancy, Banking, Secretarial Practice and such other courses require well-written standard textbooks. But wherever these courses are offered in regional medium, the problem is compounded by the non-availability of good textbooks written in the regional language. It is only recently that attempts are being made to have necessary textbooks prepared by experts in respective areas. But keeping in view the disrepute that textbook writers have brought upon themselves in recent times, for reasons best known to themselves, it looks we have still miles to go before we achieve success in this venture.

Problem of Syllabus Formulation

Formulation of functional syllabi has always been a problem in our conditions. It is argued that the syllabi for technical and vocational courses always tend to be rather extensive and teachers are often at doldrums as to what should be taught in the class. The syllabi at the national level are, no doubt, framed in consultation with subject experts in respective fields. It definitely saves time and money and is also necessary for bringing about uniformity but it may not be acceptable and adaptable to satisfy local needs all the time. Vagueness and obscurity can be avoided if competent teachers, who are better conversant with student needs i.e., employment requirements, formulate the syllabi locally. Further, there must be proper coordination at every stage. Else, there is always a possibility of the creeping in of duplication and overlapping. Such actions may stand in the way of preparing meaningful and effective course materials in areas like marketing and salesmanship, banking etc. It is true that all teachers teaching technical and vocational courses cannot be involved in the exercise of preparing course materials every year. It can be very effectively done by rotation as well as providing for regional representation of competent and experienced teachers. It is important because proper balancing of theory and practical is necessary to make the syllabi balanced and unbiased. Technical and Vocational courses need more practical activities and therefore one or one and a half hour practical per week per paper, which is quite common in most vocational institutes, is in reality far too inadequate and disproportionate keeping in view the nature of the course.

Problems of Student Selection

General publicity and advertisement should be enough for the students to seek admission in vocational or any other courses. Students have to be made aware of the future prospects that a particular course has in store for them. An institute or a course of study, which cannot guarantee a secure future after the completion of the programs it offers, fails to attract students for admission. And parents, for certain reasons, are not quite willing to send their daughters for a course in nursing.

Moreover, they don't feel it worth forcing their children to go for courses they are not interested in. Only those who score very low marks at the school final and fail to get seats in general courses in academic colleges show the desire to take up vocational courses. But then, since only the qualitatively poor students get admitted, the performance remains equally poor in most cases. Moreover, the training of such students happens to be a difficult job for the teachers. However, even if such substandard students are attracted to these courses in large numbers and the institute can offer quality education and training, it is well and good.

The desire for higher education is natural and the selection of a particular course should be the personal choice of the students. But we cannot expect the academically brilliant students to take up vocational courses in the prevailing conditions and get lost in the whirlpool of employment market at a tender age. We cannot either stop someone from going in for it on the ground of their remaining unemployable even after the successful completion of certain courses. But proper counseling will make the students aware of all the implications involved in choosing a particular course and help them make proper choices.

Problem of balancing Social Polarity

Only students hailing from rural areas with an agricultural background and belonging to backward communities and castes were supposed to be attracted to vocational courses in the past. This so happened because it was assumed that students who belonged to relatively poorer sections of the society, might be interested in quick gainful employment and it was believed that vocational courses had the impetus to provide this scope to them. Time has progressed and it is rather impossible to collect relevant data on rural family income of an earlier period in the present context. But information collected from past records broadly represents the respective income groups, which showed an increasing tendency to opt for vocational courses. To the extent that these courses were expected to train them for gainful employment within a short period, everything was well and good; but in due course, it was found that they were increasingly denied access to high income positions because of the limited prospects of the vocations, which they were compelled to take up on completion of their training. The result being that they had no option but to remain in the lower and middle-income level, which has formed a class of its own i.e., the middle-income group and the lower-income group. Moreover, it is an undeniable fact that vocational courses are primarily expected to prepare students to become skilled workers and not bosses. This is in contrast to general education, which has increasingly become a strong channel of social and economic mobility.

Problems from Students' Perspective

Students face various problems while they are studying. Students' problems may be mainly classified into two categories:

Training problems

Training programs can't be effectively carried out due to certain physical and technical problems of the institution. Such problems affect the students psychologically and therefore, have a pernicious affect on the teaching-learning process. Some such problems are:

A. **Lack of proper laboratory facilities:** In many places it is found that technical and vocational institutions and colleges have laboratories but do not possess the necessary equipments. Students are required to go to other institutions for laboratory works even during examinations. Institutions opting for science and vocational stream should have a laboratory of their own. The area and accommodation of laboratories depends on the average number of students taking the subject. Everything cannot be dumped where the practical is held. So, a well-furnished spacious storeroom of at least 80 to 120 sq.ft. has to be arranged.

B. **Lack of workshop facilities:** Vocational institute carries no meaning if it does not have a full-fledged workshop of its own. Students cannot be asked to go to other workshops every now and then for practical works. Whenever needed, the students should get the opportunity to handle tools, do manual works and understand the value of the dignity of labour. Attention should also be given to safety and health factors while planning workshops. The focus of attention should concentrate on the following components:

- Adequate space for each activity
- Adequate light and ventilation
- Adequate fire precaution measures
- Proper electrification
- Use of proper floor surface material
- Water facilities
- Other security measures

C. **Lack of well-constructed building:** An ideally constructed school/college campus should comprise of an assembly hall – a multipurpose room, which can be put to various uses as per requirements. A well-constructed assembly hall can function as a hall for dramas and film shows, an exhibition room, a lecture theatre, an examination hall, hall for indoor games and annual functions, common room, a gymnasium, a meditation center or even as a community center. It should ensure easy access to students as well as public but it should preferably be located on the ground floor and isolated from the noisy region – free from parking zone and other disturbances. If the building is not constructed logically, there is every possibility of noise pollution, which affects pupils' concentration and they might be mentally disturbed.

The following guidelines can be followed for planning the construction of the building:

o Draw up a master plan initially for the site as a whole. This will facilitate the future expansion of the building, which is, to say a truism, vitally essential for the development of the institution.

o Construct the nucleus first. Starting the building with a nucleus and then proceeding step by step for expansion as per requirements will, in the long run, involve less expenditure but provide maximum facilities.

o Enlist community helps, which can be taken for developmental activities of the institution.

o Prepare capital outlay in advance for residential purposes.

o Consider the prospect of introducing the two-shift system to cope with heavy enrolment, if required in future. Future requirements, if it comes unexpectedly, will create problems. Pre-planning is therefore essential as well as beneficial.

o Prepare an agenda in advance for raising funds (if necessary and necessary will always be there) for utilizing as much of built-up space as possible.

A. **Lack of necessary equipments/instruments:** For efficient functioning, the school or college office should be well furnished with latest modern equipments. If our target is technical and vocational education, workshops and laboratories should also be well equipped with proper equipments and instruments. Grants provided for this purpose i.e., for the purchase of equipments and instruments can be utilized for the purchase of cupboards to store the equipments and small instruments. Good maintenance and proper handling will keep it in excellent condition for many years. Laboratory assistants and mechanics should be carefully selected and appointed. They need to be qualified, which means that they should know their subjects well; but at the same time they should be well behaved and sincere in their job, as they will be required to work with the pupils.

B. **<u>Lack of adequate space for building as well as playground</u>:** Most schools and colleges suffer due to the shortage of accommodation. The following requirements have to be kept in mind in selecting a site for any school or college – vocational or otherwise:

o Sufficient building space for future expansion.
o Sufficient space for playground.
o Sufficient space for community activities – recreational or otherwise.
o Sufficient space for community facilities i.e., a health club and a clinic for emergency.
o Sufficient space for constructing quarters for teachers with garden facilities.
o Space for feeding facilities for teachers and students.

The school/college campus should have adequate space — sufficiently enough to satisfy the requirements of curricular as well as co-curricular activities. The importance of playground in colleges and particularly in schools cannot be refuted. It is a necessity for the all round development of students' personality. In this context Wellington's remark is worth remembering, *"The Battle of Waterloo was won on the playing fields of Eton."* If it is really so, how big the field could be!

C. **<u>Lack of competent laboratory technicians and mechanics</u>:**

Laboratory assistants and mechanics should be carefully selected and appointed. They need to be qualified, which means that they should know their subjects well; but at the same time they should be well behaved and sincere in their job, as they will be required to work with the pupils. They should be hard-working, as students need adequate training in practical work. Inefficient and inept technicians become problem creators for the students.

All these points speak of the need for the creation of the required infrastructure. It can't be denied that provision of adequate infrastructure involves huge expenditure, which may not be possible for an institution to meet without a substantial grant from the government. The Directorate responsible for the disbursement of funds may, if it so desires make out a case for higher allotments for at least those courses, which involve larger investments in terms of infrastructure, and make necessary efforts to obtain bigger grants from the Government if necessary.

Post-Training Problems

Vocational courses are devised with a single-minded aim to prepare students straightway for jobs or for self-employment. But few students, once they get the diploma or degree, seem to be interested in self-employment. They prefer to go for a salaried job instead as white-collar workers. The other way, very few of our students seem to have the knack or ability to take up self-employment. Moreover, self-employment in most cases, involves finance and it is not possible for all students to manage the required amount for the purpose. State Financial Corporations in Assam as in other states have, no doubt, received necessary directives from the Government to advance loans for vocationally trained persons for self-employment. Nationalized Banks also have, in the meanwhile, recognized the vocationally trained students as technical entrepreneurs for advancing loans under self-employment schemes. But some financially poor students don't dare to go for loans for fear of not being able to repay the loan in case his venture fails. They prefer to opt for jobs. Further, girl students don't dare to go for self-employment for obvious reasons. Despite the fact that time has changed and girls have become self dependent, at times, it turns out to be really difficult for girls to take a decision on their own.

For all these reasons, students prefer going for salaried jobs. There always was, and there still is a mixed feeling among students that the moment they complete the course they would be provided jobs. But it is not usually so. And this gives rise to desperation and frustration and thereby it leads to adverse social problems and dilemmas.

Main Problems of Polytechnic Education in India

Not only in ITIs but in Government Polytechnics as well, the diploma programmes have continued to deteriorate over the years and the skill components remain neglected due to lack of awareness and understanding. The organizations employing the diploma holders are confused as they are required to train them all over again in basic skills. This predicament points towards the following key issues faced by the polytechnic education system as well: -

1. Non-availability of courses in new and emerging areas.
2. Inadequate infrastructure facilities and outdated equipment.
3. Dearth of competent and skilled teachers
4. Lack of adequate financial resources
5. Lack of well-designed state policies for training and retraining of faculty and staff
6. Lack of flexibility and autonomy to the institutions
7. Lack of adequate industry-institute participation
8. Lack of adequate Research and Development
9. Obsolete Curricula.

Options for conceivable solution —

Re-engineering the whole system of education with a judicious amalgamation of vocational education may be one of the conceivable solutions. Public Service Commission can alter its recruitment policy and make it a point to see that those who have diplomas and degrees in technical and vocational courses from good and approved institutes / colleges would be given preference in recruitment. The same should be applicable in all other selections for appointment. Candidates having professional degrees and diplomas with sufficient practical works and projects to their credit should be given preference for placements. But this is not done in most cases as a result of which, very often professionally superior candidates happen to be deprived of their legitimate rights. This should not happen. The Commission should make it specifically clear that the cadre and recruitment rules have been amended to recognize technical and vocational courses and henceforth give it topmost priority in selection of candidates for certain jobs. It is only then that the students will be enthused to enroll themselves in vocational courses with the belief that jobs will somehow be available at least to the few who top the list. But there is another aspect, which has to be taken seriously. Students should not develop the notion that the Principal is responsible for finding jobs for them after they complete their courses.

Students should also realize that job opportunities cannot be made available to each and everyone. Try you must for a job but shouldn't waste your time and energy for a very long time looking for jobs only. At the same time you should have zeal to improve yourself, equip yourself in a better way for better job prospects and, if necessary, go for higher education for that. There are cases where even suitable candidates i.e., successful diploma holders are not selected even for temporary jobs on various pretexts. They are told that their courses could not be recognized because there is no specific government directive to that effect. As a result students who have successfully completed their courses and should have been suitably employed are compelled to go for further studies even at the cost of financial constraints in the family. Such students are sometimes found to take up general courses at this stage. Universities do justice to them by at least permitting them to join courses in the Arts stream. Nevertheless, they can't but be mentally depressed because they are haunted by the fact that their technical training has been nothing more than wastage of time, money and energy. Moreover, a course in humanities or Social Sciences will be simply meaningless for students who have completed courses like X-Rays or Printing Technology or even Health Engineering. Therefore, it would be justified if students were allowed to take up higher study in the relevant courses. For example, a student with a diploma in X-Ray may take up Radiology; a student with Secretarial Practice Diploma may go for a Commerce course and one having a Diploma in Pharmacy may go for B.Pharma. It is in this aspect that the universities can be called upon to play a very constructive role in the years to come.

Other points to focus on:

- Studies have shown that the number of students for long term vocational courses is declining, mainly in ITIs. The training policy should be focused on the changing job market in order to attract young people but it lacks the required focus in this direction. Institutes need to be provided more autonomy than ever before and they should have profuse market linked infrastructure. It is also equally important that job creation must be done locally to help create regional balances of trained manpower in the coming days.

- Study has revealed that financial support for public ITIs is extremely poor in India compared to China, USA and other developed countries. Funds are so streamlined in those countries that the share directly goes to the upgrading of vocational training systems so as to achieving global excellence. It is true that things are moving ahead in India as well and with the introduction of the National Skill Development Mission, it is anticipated that conditions might get better in the Twelfth 5-year Plan. But it is also desirable to have effective device to raise funds privately from other sources as well for up-gradation of the ITIs.

- ITIs must focus on providing new courses and formally well-trained staff should be engaged for conducting the workshops. The department should take it as a fundamental challenge to formally train workers and make them familiar with the latest technologies for the crafts industry.

- Lack of accountability and proper training as well as poor supply management are also major problems for ITI's not only in Assam but in other parts of India as well.

- There are innumerable institutes imparting vocational training in our country but they lack co-ordination and hence it is practically impossible to get correct information about this sector from a single source. A central database should be instituted from where full access on vocational education and training system from school level to ITIs and ITCs would be possible.

- Well-trained and competent Para-medical persons are few in the countryside i.e., the rural sector. Better late than never, Policy makers and respective departments should focus on the paramedical vocational studies, so that the number of trained paramedical workers can be increased as required..

- An accredited Central Technical and Vocational Education and Training Standardization System should be constituted for maintaining the quality of vocational education. It is quality which can enhance credibility of vocationally trained persons in the industry.

- Proper re-orientation of vocational courses is vitally essential to attract more students from school level for technical and vocational education.

- Provision should be made to facilitate vocationally trained individuals to get the benefits of R&D.

Directorate of Vocational / Technical Education: Its accountability

The Directorate of Technical Education (DTE) can do a lot in helping students become career conscious and pursue the career of their choice with persistent zeal and resolute determination. In the process of setting desirable criteria for the formation and activities of different departments under the directorate, the problem of accountability also arises. The departments can be basically accountable for its activities to:

> the directorate directly

> the society or community which entrust its young ones to the care and education prescribed by the concerned departments under the directorate.

> the students who opt for the course designed under the advice and supervision of the directorate.

This makes it clear that the DTE itself is, to a great extent, obliged to account for all the ways the departments function. It should, therefore, inspire its subsidiary departments including institutes/colleges through its own conduct worth imitating. It should be able to provide a systematic, well-planned approach in order to successfully guide students and adults as they make choices for future education and careers. This august body has such an immense power that if it intends it can

o help schools equip students and adults with the skills necessary to easy and flawless transition into post-secondary education, or any other work whatsoever, while understanding the need for life-long learning and career development.

o act as a vitally essential component to help individuals connect academic coursework with their future career, which allows for improvements in academic achievement and performance, and career exploration and development.

o organize both academics and career education into a practical program for workforce preparation, enriching the coursework by making it more rigorous, challenging, and more pertinent for better career options.

o promote the wide variety of secondary as well as post-secondary options to help each individual choose and recognize the path that will provide the most successful level and type of training for their future goals and contribution in the work they do.

o provide students and adults with the necessary tools and resources to actively participate in the career development process by understanding their options,

o creating a plan for coursework, laying out goals, and accessing the information they need to make intelligent and well thought-out decisions for the future.

o generate a positive and thoughtful environment for self-discovery, and effective and informative planning, leading to more lifelong career satisfaction and success.

o open the door to career information, knowledge, and skills and provide the program to which students and adults prepare for the future.

Director of Technical and Vocational Education can play a considerably significant role in shaping the country's workforce and economy of tomorrow.

The directorate, to be able to function effectively and realise the above objectives should have the aptitude to recognize the diverse needs, behaviours, backgrounds, and preferences of students and the community by creating an environment for providing necessary guidance and preparation for goals, plans, and individual pursuit for realizing the respective dream choice. It should also be dynamic, flexible, and responsive to the ever-changing needs and advances of technology and its impact on vocational education, the workforce as well as the economy, incorporating innovative methods, ideas, and resources to make vocational and technical education relevant and potentially employable.

+++++++++++++++++++

VI

VOCATIONAL GUIDANCE
[in the Context of Vocationalisation]

Vocational Guidance – Its significance

The information as to what kind of work will be most suitable for a person keeping in view his abilities and aptitudes is known as vocational guidance. Vocational guidance is also called Career Guidance a part of the selection process of employees – a pre-recruitment process for new employees who have not had any work experience beforehand. A few functional definitions of vocational guidance are spelt out below:

Dale Yoder -- *"Vocational guidance refers to the inevitable direction given to the care of new employees in the selection process and in their assignment to particular types of work."*

John D. Crites -- *"Vocational guidance is a facilitative process, a service rendered to the individual to aid him in choosing and adjusting to an occupation."*

National Vocational Guidance Association -- *"Vocational guidance is a process of assisting the individual to choose an occupation, prepare for it, enter up on and progress on it".*

Vocational Guidance is basically the art of giving advice and counseling techniques to assist job seekers in taking decisions. The focus of career counseling is generally on issues such as career search, career change, career growth and other career related issues. Vocational guidance program may constitute advising candidates as to what type of job they should decide on. It is of paramount importance that the right person is selected for the right job.

Definition of vocational guidance differs worldwide, and even creates confusion with the term 'counseling'. Vocational guidance, *career guidance*, *career counseling* and *careers advice* are used to mean the same thing and due to the extensive reference among academics and practitioners around the world, *career guidance and counselling* have become quite common.

Principles of Vocational Guidance:

The formulation of the main principles of career choice depends on a sound framework for career and technical education. Over the years, the concept known as vocational guidance and education, has grown and evolved to become a focus in our schools, workforce and government. The government has understood the importance and need of career and technical education in our society and has made sufficient progress in this area. But comparatively speaking, hardly any existing vocational programs in our country follow the social and economical principles outlined in this work. Even the best public school will have its deficiencies; but still, some such schools demonstrate that even with few material resources, it is possible to make vocational education an invaluable asset for children, the communities and the nation. Some of the fundamental principles to be followed in letter and spirit are:

(1) Vocational guidance process should be objective and must be based on facts.

(2) The approach should be convincing and practical and at no point force or intimidation should be used.

(3) The candidate should be made conversant with all possible job opportunities and he should have the liberty to make his own choice.

Conventional Procedures

(i) Information about the candidate is collected from the candidate himself, his teachers and his parents.

(ii) Additional information about the candidate can be known by giving him certain tests like aptitude test and personality tests.

(iii) His health, height, weight etc., should also be given due weightage.

On the basis of the information gathered, the candidate will be guided as to which job is best suitable for him. In actual fact, vocational guidance is needed at the school and college level to guide and help students to choose their subjects (science, commerce or arts) according to their interests and aptitudes.

Presently this guidance is provided by parents and teachers but it is always better if it is given by some skilled expert who is generally a psychologist. In advanced countries, professional psychologists are selected and appointed in educational institutions for providing vocational guidance.

Benefits of Vocational Guidance:

The following benefits can be accumulated from methodical vocational selection:

(a) The candidate obtains motivational satisfaction after being selected for the job of his choice.

(b) It opens the door for better industrial relationships.

(c) The employment ratio would be reduced to minimum.

(d) It shows the way for overall competence and increased output..

Vocational Education and Vocational Guidance

Both are so closely inter-related that one is not complete without the other. Vocational education will be a futile pursuit if it is not followed by an adequately satisfactory program of vocational education. Yet again, in actual fact, no program of vocational education can be effectively implemented if it is not preceded by vocational guidance. "Vocational education without vocational guidance is much like trying to make an automobile crank shaft out of any bar of metal that comes handy without first determining whether it is suitable for the purpose. Vocational guidance without vocational education is like selecting with great care a bar of steel suitable for a crank shaft without providing proper facilities for subjecting it to the process of forming, tempering and gauging necessary for the purpose. Both vocational guidance and vocational education are necessary to a successful transfer from school to working life," – It is so well said by George E. Mayers.

The formulation of the main principles of career choice depends on a sound framework for career and technical education. Over the years, the concept known as vocational guidance and education, has grown and evolved to become a focus in our schools, workforce and government. The government has understood the importance and need for career and technical education in our society and has made sufficient progress in this area. But comparatively speaking, hardly any existing vocational programs in our country follow the social and economical principles outlined in this work. Even the best public school will have its deficiencies; but still, some such schools demonstrate that even with few material resources, it is possible to make vocational education an invaluable asset for children, the communities and the nation.

Vocational Guidance in India:

In India, it is conventional for employment exchanges to provide vocational guidance to youth without any basic work experience and adults with specific work experience.

In order to motivate and redirect educated youth to channels of gainful employment, vocational guidance and career counseling agenda of the Directorate General of Employment and Training have been updated and restructured. Career study centres and the Central Institute for Research and Training provide career literature to provide necessary information about occupational orientation of the youth and other aspirants for suitable employment.

The Central Institute for Research and Training in Employment Services (CIRTES) under the Director General of employment and training is responsible for imparting training to job aspirants. It is also occupied with the responsibility of conducting research in diverse areas and fields of employment segment.

Challenges

One of the major challenges coupled with career counseling is motivating people to engage in the course of action. It has been acknowledged that career advice is something that is extensively conducted all the way through a series of formal and informal roles. In addition to career counselors it is also common for psychologists, teachers, managers, trainers and Human Resource (HR) specialists to give formal support to career choices. Similarly it is also common for people to seek informal support from family members, peers and seniors within their own profession as well as their teachers and that way it is like bypassing the procedure i.e., seeking counseling from career professionals. Today more and more people rely on career web portals to seek advice on resume writing and handling interviews; as also to carry on projects and research on various professions and companies. The most convenient thing today is that it has even become possible to take vocational assessments online and prove one's employability.

U.S. Commission on National Aid to Vocational Education had declared way back in 1914, "There is a great crying need of providing vocational education to conserve and develop the resources of the Nation, to promote a more productive and a prosperous agriculture, to prevent the waste of home labour, to supplement apprenticeship; to increase the wage earning power of our productive workers, to meet the increasing demand for trained workmen; and to offset the increased cost of living. Vocational education is, therefore, needed as a wise business investment for our nation, because our national prosperity and happiness are at stake and our position in the markets of the world cannot otherwise be maintained." This declaration made way back in 1914 holds good for our country today even after more than seven decades.

The formulation of the main principles of career choice depends on a sound framework for career and technical education. Over the years, the concept known as vocational guidance and education, has grown and evolved to become a focus in our schools, workforce and government. The government has understood the importance and need for career and technical education in our society and has made sufficient progress in this area. But comparatively speaking, hardly any existing vocational programs in our country follow the social and economical principles outlined in this work. Even the best public school will have its deficiencies; but still, some such schools demonstrate that even with few material resources, it is possible to make vocational education an invaluable asset for children, the communities and the nation.

The number of students, who attend vocational courses in India at the secondary stage, is almost certainly the lowest in the world. Studies have revealed that in West Germany, about 70 per cent students at the secondary stage opt for vocational courses which prepare them for a career-oriented life all through. In Japan, this percentage is about 60. The position is the same in almost all the advanced and industrial countries worldwide. But in India, most recent study has revealed that only about 3.5 per cent of students enrolled at the secondary level of education pursue vocational courses. Earlier, the percentage was just 2.5 due to certain innovative initiatives undertaken by the government and the changed mindset of the new generation. But the enrolment data is still too poor and speaks for itself the gravity of the situation. This poses as a serious challenge for the country and demands that vocational guidance should work as a facilitative process to be able to bring about the required change in the system.

Roles of Vocational Guidance Activities

Vocational guidance activities of a school, as already discussed above, have a dual role to play in effective implementation of the scheme of Vocationalisation of Education:

1. Providing required guidance to students, parents and faculty members in respect of educational and vocational choice.

2. Helping in actual administration and smooth functioning of all programs.

3. Imparting lessons on the values of dignity of labour and other desirable attitudes towards manual work.

4. Providing a platform to be able to understand the world of work and the principles involved in different forms of work. Such information will be disseminated through a number of exploratory and career education activities like class projects, career albums, preparation of charts and posters, visits, field trips and other kinds of exposure to work and skills required in various forms of work.

5. Taking into consideration that a lot of flexibility exists at +2 stage, proper stratification of students according to the provisions of facilities in the school and according to the preferences of students based on their likes and dislikes, as well as capabilities and other factors is required to be done. A lot of investigative works into the assessment activities and personality characteristics of individuals will be required. Hence the required psychological appraisal of pupils for identification of relevant data will be done by guidance counselors.

6. Considering the fact that vocational courses are terminal in nature, information relating to job openings, methods of applying and obtaining jobs, scope and opportunities for self-employment and salaried jobs etc., has to be co-ordinated with the students' future career plans.

7. The school counselor will also have the important job of helping the +2 passed-outs in finding on the job training and/or placement by working in collaboration with employers and the employment exchanges. Career

guidance activities like reviewing and discussing the applicants' qualifications and interests in relation to available employment opportunities will be required.

8. The guidance worker is expected to keep and maintain a link between pupils, educational sector and the employment sector at local, district and state level.

The National Review Committee (1978) has recommended that counseling and placement officers be appointed in clusters of three or four schools, particularly in rural areas to start with. Their function will be to advise students on the choice of elective subjects, and organize for them remedial courses to make up deficiencies in interested areas. The Committee also recommended that necessary help should be provided to students in securing proper placements by having a close contact with the related agencies.

Occupational Survey - Role of the Counselor

The NCERT document, *"Higher Secondary Education and its Vocationalisation (1976)"* proposes a survey of activities to find out employment opportunities/for an area/ unit or a district. The local employment opportunities could be exploited and imbalance between manpower shortages and surpluses in various fields of work could be reduced to minimum.

Proper linkages between the District Man-power and Employment Generation Councils, the Employers at different levels of job segment have to be established to determine the nature and scope of such surveys. The actual information and publication of such reports will help remove the imbalance between shortage and surplus in different service sectors. At the school level, counselor is the most suitable person, who, on the basis of his intensive training and background in collection of occupational information and related skills can help plan the contents and format of the information to be collected in the occupational survey.

Infrastructure Facilities

The conduct of occupational surveys helps in selecting and locating the appropriate vocational courses and on-the-job training, but the actual administration of the programmes has to be co-ordinated with the manpower planning and other statutory bodies and the employing agencies within the community. The school counselor will establish such links as may be necessary, to co-ordinate the programmes and ensure the smooth functioning of the system. He will keep in touch with the statutory bodies like Nursing Council, Pharmacy Council, ICMR boards of Technical Education, the ITIs and the Directorate General of Employment and Training. The Programme of Action 1986 has recommended setting up of National Level and State Level Councils for Vocational Education which would be Apex bodies with the membership of all statutory bodies. The school guidance counselors could also be a part of these bodies; and by acting as a bridge between educational administrators and these statutory bodies they can prove instrumental in the process of establishing a relationship between education, the working life and the community as a whole.

Development of Vocational Skills

Basic Objectives of the Vocationalisation of Education essentially envisages development of vocational skills in the students, thereby making them more gainfully employable either through self employment or wage employment in vocations of their choice. Between 50% and 80% of the total instructional time for the study and practice of vocational electives has been recommended by various committees on vocationalisation. It is suggested that a reasonable amount of this allotted time be earmarked for Career Education which is aimed at providing such educational experiences to the students as would 'facilitate his career development and preparation for the world of work'. It is also proposed that the guidance worker may take these classes on Career Education in collaboration with vocational teachers who may be full-time or part-time representatives from various industries. Vocational education subjects are mainly skill subjects and the teacher teaching these subjects should know the pedagogy and skills in affective training besides vocational training. The teacher and the guidance worker both will have to see that the students have developed required vocational skills as well as the systematic and orderly manipulative skills. Such work habits approximating to dignity of labour, diligence and perseverance, co-operative attitude, quick decision making ability, initiative, planning etc., are the effective components of vocational and career education, development of which will be the primary concern of a guidance counselor.

+++++++++++++++++++++

VII

NEED OF A CHANGED MINDSET

Time has changed. Children are no more traditional in their career choices. Today, if you ask what they want to be when they grow up, their answers will no longer be doctors, teachers or engineers. Definitely, their choices will be different. If you happen to ask secondary / senior secondary level students what they intend to do after they finish school, you'll get a range of answers, which depicts a sudden change in their likes and dislikes for certain jobs. Today, most students intend to take up only such courses, which have huge job prospects in the present context. Courses like bar management and beauty parlour management, which were looked down upon in the past, are emerging as hot middle-class career options. There was a time when anyone venturing into these sectors were considered proportionately ordinary or average category of people. But these mindsets are fast changing and more and more youngsters are taking up these careers and doing well. The job market today is so variegated and dynamic that there are thousand and one options for job seekers. Students are also aware of the changing trends and ready to try new and challenging avenues. With the change of time parents too seem to be more or less convinced of the idea that success comes to him who has the courage to tread on unexplored zones. The majority of them today don't find fault with their children's desire to look for new horizons away from home.

The important thing is that one has to acquire the requisite qualifications, abilities and perfections in the chosen field to get the best of it. There is immense scope for good placement opportunities for those who are academically talented. But others can also be either self-employed and do independent work or act as consultants in different firms. One gets the scope to groom and equip himself in a better way for better opportunities. As in everything else, here too a lot of practice is necessary and one has to keep on learning the latest skills and techniques involved in the job he or she opts for.

A very important factor that has popularized these alternative careers is the likelihood of a reasonable pay package within a very short time span. There are jobs, which can fetch you, anything between Rs.7000 to Rs.1lakh a month. But one has to be really good in his job to be considered eligible for a package of Rs.50,000 and above. There are people who doubt the usefulness of institutes offering diploma courses and not academic degrees. Still there are parents who seem to be seriously worried about their kids taking up non-professional works of the type spoken above.

Is it because we've the tendency to emphasize on academic degrees awarded by universities? But how far do the present universities contribute towards making education a wholesome experience for its degree holders? But there are institutes, which strive on idealizing life and providing the type of education, which aims at building better citizens and shaping a better world. In these institutes there is an atmosphere, which inspirits the students to become dreamers, achievers and winners. In India there are millions of graduates and under-graduates doing nothing. So, there is nothing wrong in doing a diploma course right after Class X or XI or XII, if the course is geared to the job market.

Nowadays, there is an increasing demand for vocational courses and students can't but be ever willing to undertake a Certificate Course in a good institute if they are properly guided and made to believe that it will help them get a well-paid job. A good Guidance and Counseling Clinic can be of great help to these undergraduates if they intend to discontinue their regular study after school final and go for vocational type of courses. Many private as well as affiliated career institutes are doing this job. 'Emphasis on life' is what these institutes bank upon. They keep their pledge and so in spite of being costly, they attract students. Universities too can very well highlight its functioning by drawing the essence of epitomizing life which can be the most appealing feature for the literate folk who come here from different parts of the country to shape their destiny.

Education cannot create employment but made inter-disciplinary and skill-based, it can become career-oriented and life related and create virtually potential persons fit for employment. It should have a direct relevance to the needs and requirements of real-life job situations, which means that courses should be need-based, job-oriented as well as it should have enough potentiality to generate self-employment which is another way of saying that the process of education should be directly linked with production and employment.

Some may say career and education is related and others may deny the same. Surveys and innovative projects conducted by many reputed firms indicate that they are co-related. One may not be highly qualified or may not have a university degree as such, but may be placed in a high position. The other, who is the product of a university, may terribly fail as a career launcher.

Education has no barrier for anyone. No matter how old you are, you are never too old to learn new things. In the same way, you are never too old to receive career education and give the impression that you deserve better placement and better package. Every one of us has a tendency to look for better options, with better package and better job conditions. Not everyone knows for sure what they need to be to grow up. But we must have a dream and we should strive to realize that dream. Certainly the changing world economy, and how that affects careers, comes into play here. It is important therefore, for the students to know as to what the main reasons are for which education should be the vanguard of the career decision-making process. What is important is that as students you need to have an inherent desire to acquire knowledge and an intrinsic urge for career development.

It is for this reason that whether one opts for Degree/Diploma in Business Administration, Law/Criminal justice, Computer Engineering, Fashion Technology, Information Technology, Informatics or whatsoever, he has to make sure that he is flying out with colors, so that it will provide required force and power in his career. A degree from an accredited university or having a proper college degree also helps to gear for more reputation, and yes, it helps a lot in case he is looking for a promotion. Once he is in to a profession, he should make sure that he is choosing a course that is related and useful for that profession. This helps in promotion, increment, and overall professional growth.

The trend in present-day vocational education is to shift away from the use of the word 'vocational' to label skill-based programs. Most state universities and technical and engineering institutes have selected a broader term, although a few use vocational technical education. There is an increasing tendency in India and abroad in recent times to follow the lead of the national vocational education organizations and have adopted the term career and vocational education as well as career and technical education. There are, of course, variations and terms like career and technology education and professional-technical education, and several states in the US have very sensibly included the word workforce in describing these programs. The changes in terminology reflect a viably changing economy, in which technical careers have increasingly become the basis of the nation's all-round growth, development and prosperity.

The term career education first became popular in the 1970s and when it was at its height of acceptability, it was distinguished from vocational education by its emphasis on general employability and adaptability skills applicable to all occupations, while vocational education was primarily concerned with occupational skill training for specific occupations. Basic definition of career education definitely remains appropriate even today.

The purpose of career and technical/vocational education is to provide a foundation of skills that enable high school students to be gainfully employed – either as a full-timer or part-timer. A part-timer gets plenty of time to continue education or training and improve himself for a better job or a promotion. Nearly two-thirds of all graduates in vocational and technical programs enter some form of occupation and prove quite productively.

Over the years, Vocational/ Technical Education, which was earlier referred to as vocational guidance and education in US and other countries, has grown and evolved to become a focus in our schools, workforce, and government. This has happened because with the change of time we have understood the importance and need for career and technical/vocational education in our society.

Rationale behind considering career and technical education (CTE) as the vanguard of career decision-making process:

- CTE provides a systematic and practical approach in order to successfully guide students and adults as they make choices for future education and careers.
- CTE helps schools and workforce centres equip students and adults with the skills necessary to flawlessly shift into post-secondary education or any other productive activity, while understanding the need for life-long learning and career development.
- CTE serves as a critical component to helping individuals connect academic coursework with their future career, which allows for improvements in academic achievement and performance, and career exploration and development.
- CTE organizes both academics and career education into a practical programme for workforce preparation, uplifting the level of rigorous, challenging, and relevant coursework, and leading to better and more advanced preparation.
- CTE promotes the wide variety of post-secondary options to help each individual choose and recognize the path that will provide the most successful level and type of training for their future goals and contribution in work.
- CTE provides students and adults with the necessary tools and resources to actively participate in the career development process by understanding their options, creating a plan for coursework, laying out goals,

and accessing the information they need to make knowledgeable decisions for the future.

- CTE creates a positive, thoughtful environment for self-discovery as well as effective and informative planning, leading to more lifelong career satisfaction and success.

- CTE recognizes the diverse needs, behaviours, backgrounds, environments, and preferences of students and adults by creating an approach that allows for individual guidance and preparation for goals, plans, and dreams.

- CTE poses as a dynamic, flexible, and receptive medium to the ever-changing needs and advances of technology, education, the workforce and the economy, incorporating all possible innovative methods, ideas, and resources to keep career and vocational education relevant and up to date in modern context.

- CTE opens the door to career information, knowledge, and skills and provides the program to which students and adults prepare for the future.

Ultimately, Career and Vocational Education, if well-designed, plays a major role in shaping the global workforce and economy of tomorrow. This gives good reason to establish how relevant vocational schooling is in today's highly competitive job market.

Relevance of Vocational schooling in today's Competitive Job Market

Vocational studies, as in the west, are fast becoming popular in India as well, with more people opting for technical and vocational courses. It is true that every student may not have the aptitude for science, law, banking, medicine, engineering etc. With vocational studies, students get a chance to make a career out of an activity they really enjoy and would be blissfully happy to do what they cherish.

We all know why students opt for conventional academic courses in banking, law, medicine, engineering etc, because we have been made to think that way. But there are certain valid reasons why tertiary vocational education provides the perfect alternative for students who are looking for an education that will suitably prepare them not just for national job market but truly speaking, for the highly competitive international job market as well. At the national level, the nature and scope of its employability may be limited to some extent. The most important reason why you should look into vocational training for your career education is that it has a very job-specific approach. The subjects, faculty, teaching pedagogy, all are aimed at helping students secure jobs immediately after they graduate. Compulsory training/apprenticeship period, practically useful projects and assignments equip the students in a better way to secure jobs after they complete their course of study. However, placement assistance needs to be given top priority by planners, administrators and educationists.

No economy is recession-proof, as even the most developed countries around the world have realized it only very recently. There are times when managers, executives, and a huge chunk of the private sector workforce face the danger of losing their jobs, and having their careers freeze mid-track. Vocational courses, on the other hand, give students the option of being self-employed. This means that even if the global economy slows down, you will still have at least job security, and the threat of the dreaded pink slip will not be looming large on your head. The only thing is you should have the spirit and urge to go ahead and not freeze.

With the economy getting global, the job market has also become increasingly competitive. Vocational courses facilitate acquiring key skills that cross international boundaries and help students secure jobs in any part of the world. A photographer, or a designer for instance, needn't any more work within national boundaries. Their talent and skills make them well-resourced for jobs in the international market.

There is no dearth of career opportunities whatsoever after your tertiary vocational education. While most begin at the trainee or apprentice level, there is tremendous scope for development and progress. Careers like photography, web designing, music and sound production, hospitality and tourism, which were earlier considered frivolous by people, are being taken very seriously these days. With formal education and training, these courses have become organized disciplines and are seen as potential goldmines of jobs, rather than just fanciful hobbies. India too has marched forward and made considerably effort to keep pace with the change of time.

Another reason as to why vocational courses are catching on is that most of them don't require you to devote 4-5 years to a college education, followed by an uncertain period of job-hunting. For mediocre students, in particular, life becomes really difficult after they graduate. The last and easiest option for them is to become a school teacher. Whether they really qualify and deserve to be on the job is nobody's business. The candidates also don't feel the need to think whether they have the competence to become a good teacher. But they opt for it and start teaching just for the sake of teaching. Most vocational courses are limited to a period of 2 years, including on-the-job training. So you save a lot of precious time and you don't have to drag yourself to unwanted tensions and anxieties. But we need to remember that the longer the duration of the course, the more valuable it becomes and makes the candidate more productive, more dynamic and more valuable for the employer and the organisation.

The hands-on training experience that tertiary vocational education provides, proves to be very practical in the high-pressure work environment today, where there are absolutely no fixed rules, binding the employee to one particular region. New challenges, pressures, transfers to different departments and countries altogether are common in the work-environment today, and vocational education indisputably prepares the students for these, in a much better way than any academic 4-5 year college degree can.

Teacher Competency – A Vital factor

Vocational education, to say a truism, is basically a technical training course, which prepares students for careers in manual and non academic fields. Vocational training is relevant to trade industries where a college degree may not be required, but hands-on training is imperative. Teaching vocational education at the high school or trade school level requires demonstrated expertise in a particular field and in some cases an associate or bachelor degree. Many vocational educators teach in order to develop a new generation of masters in a particular field.

High School

High school vocational and technical teachers teach and manage the school's vocational program. You must have a four-year degree in education, state approval and a background in a vocational field to become a faculty in a technical or vocational school. Most vocational courses are taught on-site at the high school, such as auto mechanics or welding. Students learn basic techniques, vocational terminology and general field application. For example, students embarking upon a career in the medical assistance field will learn basic medical terminology needed to take blood pressure, measure blood sugar and conduct other general medical tests. Students are taught how to apply basic knowledge to actual situations in class through role play activities and testing.

The curriculum should be well devised where it can provide students the needed scope during the last months in high school to spend in the field learning additional techniques from vocational professionals. Students, who take additional courses at a local trade school or elsewhere to enrich their classroom experience should be given due credits. High school vocational educators should frequently monitor the off-site and on-site vocation program, student's progress and assign grades according to progress. But as ill luck would have it, students are deprived of these facilities because of the non-availability of such trade schools in our country.

Most high school vocational education teachers perform the same duties as other high school teachers. This includes all the pre-teaching, on-teaching and post-teaching activities, setting question papers and examining answer scripts and also participating in academic and non-academic meetings. But teaching vocational subject requires confirmed proficiency in that field and this has to be taken care of, if we intend to build accomplished citizens and a flourishing nation.

Trade or Technical School/ Institute

Trade or technical schools can provide students hands-on experience in a particular field of specialization. Many students, who attend trade or technical schools in lieu of college, want to acquire a skill that would help them to make it a career.

Such schools require teachers who hold a bachelor's or master's degree in their field of specialization. However, if necessary, vocational schools can hire educators based on field expertise.

For example, hotel management schools look for highly skilled chefs with industry experience to conduct courses. These schools do not require teachers who have a college degree, but instead they have to show demonstrated and proven experience as an industry leader.

Educators intending to teach in a vocational school have a variety of options. According to Vocational Schools Database, vocational and technical schools are located in all Indian states. But how efficient they are and whether they have the ability to serve a wide variety of industries are vital questions. And until and unless these questions are attended to in proper perspective, and unless there are really competent teachers to teach, the best vocational syllabus in the world would not be worth the paper it is written on.

+++++++++++++++++++

VIII

WRAPPING UP

Time changes and with it people's thoughts and attitudes also change. It is not uncommon for people to go through a life changing experience and wanting to change careers in mid stream. When we are looking for something better, and if we really intend to be there, it is vitally important that we have the appropriate education for the target of our choice. This presents a couple of challenges.

o   This is an age for specialists. Do we have the requisite qualification for our new career? If not, we will have to determine where we want to stand in life and in what way we'll have to qualify ourselves to be there. Nowadays, we can study online or attend evening classes without having to quit our job. Online degrees and diplomas are yet to be easily accepted and recognized unanimously in countries like India. We still have miles to go to understand and appreciate the need and validity of such credentials. However, again, **ONLINE** diplomas and degrees, if it comes from an accredited college or university, should be considered acceptable for jobs. All of us have our likes and dislikes. Just having the ability to locate the profession of our choice and trying to specialize in that area will open up amazing opportunities for us hitherto unexpected and unimagined.

o Likewise, when we switch our careers we may be taking a pay cut. No one starts at the top and we might need to earn our way up the ladder with our new career. This is usually worth it as we get older, because career fulfillment is more important than money. Moreover, in countries like India, government employees are usually less paid and have restricted scale and possibility for promotions and incentives. It is for such reasons that they often seem to be less inspirited to work overtime. But of course, if we know how to make ourselves and our job challenging, we may catch people's eyes and consequently the eye of the government. Things might then change for the better.

o Regardless of where we are in our life career, education is important and it is the skill education that counts. It is the skill education that moulds up a child into a potential human being and a real resource for the country. Education should be so devised as to imbibe the intrinsic value of work culture among the students.

With every passing moment, job market is becoming increasingly challenging. At the same time, this complexity brings in a lot of mental power that drives the new generation employment options at a much more exemplified way thereby leading to a comprehensive growth factor for Career Opportunities. Because of this fast changing scenario, professionals need to upgrade their basic knowledge and skills, thereby taking a pro-active step towards grasping the right job at the right time. Therefore, potential job-seekers need to get properly equipped with suitable skills, take timely advice from the right mentors and build up an appropriate CV before applying for jobs. Requisite condition for the right job is another essential component, which a professional needs to mix and match up for developing that class in excellence which in its entirety adds flavour to the career launch. And it is this which exhibits our flawless perfection. It is true to all categories of job options available.

My intention was just to probe deep into a critical pedagogy of career education as an important means to enhance vocationalisation in a really authentic sense. Today, vocational education is overwhelmingly subordinated to the economic imperatives of the nation and increasingly to the logic of global economics rather than to the moral and ethical dimensions of education. A critical pedagogy of career education offers a theoretical approach that acknowledges the significance of acquiring solid technical skills while stressing the importance of engaging students in an emancipators' dialogue in which they can talk freely about expectations, fears, and frustrations regarding the world of education and work. It also introduces students to the history of work and labour, to the struggles they face in their workplaces and to make choices among the wide-ranging systems of economic development while allowing them to work collectively, to learn from each other, and to assume positions of leadership.

We need to start by thinking about the direction we want our career to take, and then concentrate on the course of actions to find fulfillment in that career. Then we need to learn the skills we need to get ahead; and find out how to deal with the challenges we'll face, in a graceful and seemingly effortless way.

Effective learning and information skills are essential for successful professionals. Early in our career we must study a huge volume of information, simply to become effective. As we become increasingly successful, we'll need to process large volumes of documents, data and reports, just to keep up-to-date in our field.

Intensive search and experience will teach us **countless skills** that will help us do these things. The art of note-taking e.g., gives us powerful tools for recording information, concisely and effectively. The skill of reading, well-developed while at school helps increase our reading ability and the ability to think critically helps us strengthen our capability to think and reason before using the acquired skills in new situations.

Most people think that getting a right type of career education is not achievable, but on the contrary, it is much more challenging and much more attainable for those who have the will and desire to achieve something in life. Taking charge of one's career goals and going out to attain knowledge and education that he or she needs to achieve the coveted goal can be a very rewarding experience. Luckily, there are plenty of tools out there today that is geared specifically to lead us in right direction to the threshold of that education which will put and fix us in the career of our dreams if we have our dreams and the priority fixed. Time has changed and the new situation demands that one can't but help being career conscious and the journey should begin at quite an early age.

It is also vitally essential at this juncture, to probe deep into the factors that contribute to increasingly growing demand of the need for Career Education for our students in today's highly competitive job market.

The action in response can likewise be invariably simple but as already stated above; students need to focus on the following points:

o We need high-quality training in most jobs to make a quality career. None of us are born with the skills or training to perform most of the tasks that come with a career. If we want to become a doctor we are supposed to have spent 8 years or more obtaining the degree and specialized professional training necessary to enter this most demanding professional field. Without proper education and specialization one can never expect to enter this field and excel. And even if somehow he happens to be there, he will not be doing any good either to himself or to others but just continue to be there. If he wants to outshine, he needs to groom himself in a better way.

o Another example is in the field of business and management. The more qualified we are, the better our chances of being hired out of college. After all, we need to be the right choice for the right job. Along these lines the college we attend also counts. Colleges known for their graduates in business and management will provide a better opportunity to start with a better career than any academic college would. This we've to keep in mind if we have a dream career.

o The same is true to other technical and agricultural based courses. Lack of proper knowledge and skills will stand in the way of our achieving success and prosperity in whatever vocation we choose for ourselves. Employability skills and personal values are the critical tools and traits we need to succeed in the workplace — and they are such elements which we can learn, cultivate, develop, and maintain over our lifetime. Once we have identified the sought-after skills and values and assessed the degree to which we possess them, we should also remember that we need to document them and market them in our resume, cover letter, and interview answers. It is the first step for job-search success.

If we are still in high school, it is better we start with a good and experienced guidance counselor first. This is the best place for students to obtain the information necessary to find the right school/institute to get proper education and move forward in the right direction. I talk of good counselors here because it is only the good ones, who can even set up appointments for us so that we will be able to tour the school of our choice for career education.

Usually a good local newspaper is a great source for finding a job that may offer career education. Many people actually overlook the fact that there are often great listings in the classified section for careers with on-the-job training and education. This is a just the right way to learn about a career while getting education and hands-on-experience and at the same time make some money. If you are unsure of your exact career choice, this type of a job search may be just right for you. This way, you get to try out the career to see if it fits you instead of putting hours of education and classes into it just to change your direction.

One of the most popular places in the present day where people look for career education opportunities is the **Internet**. There are all kinds of useful websites on the Internet that can give you all kinds of information on different technical colleges and classes that are available for you to get the education needed for your specific career choice. Many of you will even go so far as having all kinds of tips on how to search for jobs, write a great resume, the best way to answer questions during an interview i.e., interview techniques and much more.

Armed with all of the helpful tools available today, job-seekers should have a pretty easy time with their search. Once they have their career choice fixed, these resources can hopefully help them find the education and the career that they desire and deserve. The pertinent question however is:

> ***Do we deserve what we desire? We need to think over it before we make any choice. Because time is extremely precious and the tragedy is – we don't realize this before it is too late!***

+++++++++++++++++++

ABBREVIATIONS AND ACRONYMS

AICTE   -- All India Council for Technical Education (within the MHRD portfolio)

AITT   -- All India Trade Test (administered under DGET)

ATI   -- Advanced Training Institute (within the DGET portfolio)

AVI   -- Accredited Vocational Institutes(s) (administered under NIOS)

BAT   -- Board(s) of Apprenticeship Training (administered under MHRD)

BTC   -- Basic Training Center(s) (administered under DGET)

CABE   -- Central Advisory Board for Education (within the MHRD portfolio)

CAC   -- Central Apprenticeship Council (within the DGET portfolio)

CAPART   -- Council for Advancement of People's Action and Rural Technology (within the portfolio of the Ministry for Rural Development)

CBSE   -- Central Board for Secondary Education (within the MHRD portfolio)

CII   -- Confederation of Indian Industry

COBSE   -- Council of Boards of School Education (in India)

COE   -- Centers of Excellence (under establishment in ITIs with funding from the central and state governments)

CP   -- Community Polytechnic(s) (within the MHRD portfolio)

CSS	--	Centrally Supported Scheme(s)
CSSVSE	--	Centrally Supported Scheme of Vocationalisation of Secondary Education
CSTRI	--	Central Staff Training and Research Institute (within the DGET portfolio)
CTS	--	Craftsman Training Scheme (administered under DGET)
DGET	--	Directorate General of Employment and Training (within MoLE)
EdCIL	--	Education Consultants India Ltd
FDI	--	Foreign Direct Investment
FICCI	--	Federation of Indian Chambers of Commerce and Industry
GDP	--	Gross Domestic Product
GER	--	Gross Enrollment Ratio
GOI	--	Government of India
GVA	--	Gross value added per worker
HRDF	--	Human Resources Development Fund
IABD	--	Inter American Development Bank
IAMR	--	Institute of Applied Manpower Research
ICS	--	Investment Climate Survey
ICT	--	Information Communication Technology
IIT	--	Indian Institute of Technology (within the MHRD portfolio)
IRDP	--	Integrated Rural Development Programme of Govt of India
ISCED	--	International Standard Classification of Education
ITC	--	Industry Training Center(s) (private institutions affiliated with NCVT)
ITI	--	Industry Training Institute(s) (public institutions affiliated with NCVT)

JCVE -- Joint Council for Vocational Education (within the MHRD portfolio)

JRY -- Jawahar Rozgar Yojana (a GOI scheme)

JSS -- Jan Shikshan Sansthan (Community Education Organisations)

KAM -- Knowledge Assessment Methodology

KEI -- Knowledge Economy Index

KVIC -- Khadi and Village Industries Commission

MHRD -- Ministry of Human Resource Development

MoLE -- Ministry of Labor and Employment

NAC -- National Apprenticeship Certificate (administered under DGET)

NBA -- National Board of Accreditation (within AICTE)

NCERT -- National Council for Educational Research and Training (within the MHRD portfolio)

NCTA -- National Competency Testing Agency (proposed agency within the MHRD portfolio)

NCTE -- National Council for Teacher Education

NER -- Net Enrollment Ratio

NCVE -- National Council for Vocational Education (within the MHRD portfolio)

NCVT -- National Council for Vocational Training (within the DGET portfolio)

NGO -- Non Government Organization

NIEPA -- National Institute of Educational Planning and Administration

NIIT -- National Institute of Information Technology (within the MHRD portfolio)

NIOS -- National Institute of Open Schooling (within the MHRD portfolio)

NITTTR -- National Institute for Technical Teacher Training and Research (within the MHRD portfolio)

NRF	--	National Renewal Fund (established by the GOI)
NSDC	--	National Skill Development Corporation
NTC	--	National Trade Certificate (administered under DGET)
OBE	--	Open Basic Education (offfered through NIOS)
PMRY	--	Prime Minister's Rozgar Yojana (a GOI scheme)
PSSCIVE	--	Pandit Sunderlal Sharma Central Institute of Vocational Education (administered under NCERT)
PUC	--	Pre-University Certificate
RIC	--	Related Instruction Center(s) (administered under DGET)
RPL	--	Recognition of Prior Learning
SAP	--	Structural Adjustment Program
SATS	--	Statutory Apprenticeship Training Scheme (administered in separate parts by DGET and MHRD)
SCVE	--	State Council(s) for Vocational Education (adninsitered by respective state governments)
SCVT	--	State Council for Vocational Training SDF Skills Development Fund (established in Singapore)
SSLC	--	Secondary School Leaving Certificate
STEP	--	Support to Training and Employment Program (under the portfolio of MHRD of GOI)
TAFE	--	Technical and Further Education (Australia)
TFP	--	Total Factor Productivity
UCEP	--	Underpriveleged Children's Education Program (in Bangladesh)
UGC	--	University Grants Commission (within the MHRD portfolio)
UT	--	Union Territory
VET	--	Vocational Education and Training

REFERENCES

ANNUAL REPORT: (2008) Ministry of Human Resource Development, Department of Education, India

BOTTOMS, GENE; PRESSON, ALICE; and JOHNSON, MARY. 1992. Making High Schools Work Through Integration of Academic and Vocational Education. Atlanta, GA: Southern Regional Education Board.

BROWN,P. and HESKETH, A. (2004) The Mismanagement of Talent: Employability and Jobs in the Knowledge Economy. Oxford, Oxford University Press.

BUTTON, KENNETH; COX, KENNETH; STOUGH, ROGER; and TAYLOR, SAMANTHA. 2001. The Long Term Educational Needs of a High-Technology Society. Washington, DC: 21st Century Workforce Commission.

Clarke, P. (2003). Secondary Education in India. Working Paper, World Bank.

COMMITTEE FOR ECONOMIC DEVELOPMENT RESEARCH AND POLICY COMMITTEE. 2000. Measuring What Matters: Using Assessment and Accountability to Improve Student Learning. New York: Committee for Economic Development.

DAGGETT, WILLARD R.; KRUSE, BENEDICT; and FIELDS, GARY M. 2001. Education as a Business Investment. Rexford, NY: International Center for Leadership in Education.

DAGGETT, WILLARD R., and OTT, TIMOTHY E. 1999. The Overcrowded Curriculum: Using Data to Determine Essential Skills. Rexford, NY: International Center for Leadership in Education

HIND,D. and MOSS,S. (2011) Employability Skills. 2nd Edition. Sunderland, Business Education Publishers.

JUDY, RICHARD W., and D'AMICO, CAROL. 1997. Workforce 2020: Work and Workers in the 21st Century. Indianapolis, IN: Hudson Institute.

RAVITCH, DIANE. 2000. Left Back: A Century of Failed School Reforms. New York: Simon and Schuster.

U.S. DEPARTMENT OF LABOR. 1990. The Secretary's Commission on Achieving Necessary Skills (SCANS). Washington, DC: U.S. Department of Labor. U.S. DEPARTMENT OF LABOR. 1999. Futurework: Trends and Challenges for Work in the 21st Century. Washington, DC: U.S. Department of Labor.

CLARKE, P. (2005). Technical and Vocational Education systems in Australia and India: An Experiment in Cross Cultural Learning. World Bank Working Paper.

DAHLMAN, CARL and ANUJA (2005). India and the Knowledge Economy: Leveraging Strengths and Opportunities. World Bank: Washington, D.C.

DGET. A Report of the Directorate General of Employment and Training, Ministry of Labour and Employment, India.

DGET (2003). Trade Apprenticeship in India under the Apprenticeship Training Scheme. Directorate General of Employment and Training, Ministry of Labor and Employment, India.

DGET (2003). Tracer Study of Trained Apprentices to Assess the Effectiveness of Apprenticeship Training Scheme. Directorate General of Employment and Training, Ministry of Labor and Employment, India.

FICCI (2002). Survey of Employers on Education and Skill Needs. Survey Conducted by the Federation of Indian Chamber of Commerce and Industry.

Gill, I., F. Fluitman. and A. Dar, eds. (2000). Vocational Education and Training Reforms: Matching Skills to Markets and Budgets. Oxford University Press.

ILO(2003). Industriual Training Institutes in India: The Efficiency Study Report. ILO Subregional Office for South Asia, New Delhi

Mathur, A. (2002). Skill Acquisition and the Indian Labor Force Employment and Labor Market Reforms in India. Paper presented in Consultative Workshop on Employment and Labor Market Reforms in India, mimeo. Institute of Human Development, New Delhi

Mitra, A. (2003). Training and Skill Formation for Decent Work in the Informal Sector: Case Studies from South India. ILO IFP/SKILLS Working Paper No. 8

Middleton, J., A. Ziderman, and A. V. Adams (1993). Skills for Productivity: Vocational Education and Training in Developing Countries. Oxford University Press and World Bank, Washington DC.

National Development Council Document (2008): Planning Commission India

National Policy on Education 1986 (1998): Ministry of Human Resource Development, Department of Education, India

National Conference on Technical Vocational Education, Training and Skills Development: A Roadmap for Empowerment (Dec. 2008): Ministry of Human Resource Development, Department of Education, India

Pillay, G. (2005). Singapore's Vocational Education and Training Reforms. Draft Working Paper, World Bank.

Narain, A. (2005). Labor Force Participation and its Determinants in India. Draft Working Paper prepared for the Study on Labor Markets in India

Pillay, G. (2005). Reforms in the Vocational Education and Training System in Korea. Draft Working Paper, World Bank.

Planning Commission of India (2002). Tenth Five Year Plan.

Planning Commission of India (2002). Economic Survey

Skill Formation and Employment Assurance in the Unorganised Sector (2009): National Commission for Enterprises in the Unorganised Sector.

Technical and Vocational Education and Training in India (Nov. 2008): Report compiled by Perya Short, Education Counseller (South Asia

Tan, H. and Savchenko, Y. (2005). In-Service Training in India: Evidence from the India Firm- Level Investment Climate Survey. World Bank Working Paper.

Tan, Hong. (2000). Malaysia Skill Needs Study. Washington, DC: World Bank Institute.

Unni, Jeemol and Uma Rani (2004). Technical Change and Workforce in India: Skill Biased Growth? Indian Journal of Labor Economics, Volume 47 (4).

Utz, A. (2005). India and the Knowledge Economy: The Role of Secondary Education. Draft Paper, World Bank Institute.

World Bank (2004). India: Investment Climate and Manufacturing Industry. South Asia Region, Washington, DC.

World Bank (2001). Bangladesh: Education Sector Review. A World Bank Report.

Mitra, A. (2003). Training and Skill Formation for Decent Work in the Informal Sector: Case Studies from South India. ILO IFP/SKILLS Working Paper No. 8

Middleton, J., A. Ziderman, and A. V. Adams (1993). Skills for Productivity: Vocational Education and Training in Developing Countries. Oxford University Press and World Bank, Washington DC.

MHRD (2003). Project Implementation Plan of National Program on Vcational Education and Training. Ministry of Human Resourceds Development, India.

Dr. Tilak Sharma M.A.(double), M.Ed., M.Phil.(double)., PGDTE (EFLU), CELTA (Cambridge ESOL) is a Dean at the University of Science and Technology, Meghalaya. He has more than three decades of teaching and training experience at his credit. He has travelled extensively throughout India and conducted National and International Workshops on ELT methodology, Vocational Education and Human Rights Education for generating awareness among school teachers and students in Kolkata, Bhopal, Nagpur and Mumbai. Some of his articles are published in interdisciplinary journals of national and international repute. This book should form an interesting reading particularly for teachers, researchers and administrators, who are curious about an individual's potential strength and are engrossed in innovative projects on Technical and Vocational Education and Training.